Biopharma R&D Partnerships

From David & Goliath *to* Networked R&D

Biopharma R&D Partnerships

From David & Goliath *to* Networked R&D

Robert Thong

Phizz Rx Publishing

Published by Phizz Rx Publishing, London, England, an imprint of the Phizz Rx Partnership.

First Edition 2016

ISBN: 978-0-9935181-0-2 (Pbk)
ISBN: 978-0-9935181-2-6 (Epub)
ISBN: 978-0-9935181-3-3 (Hbk)

This book is dedicated to my wife Marie,
who has been unwavering in her support
and an inspiration for how to live life.

About the Author

Robert Thong consults, speaks, and writes on business strategy, collaborations, and change in the bioscience sector. Over the past twenty-five years, he has worked with more than one hundred different pharmaceutical, biotech, medical device and healthcare organizations. During the 1990s, Robert worked in leading global management consultancies, serving multinational pharmaceutical and healthcare businesses in Europe and North America; he co-headed the Gemini Consulting (now Cap Gemini) Life Sciences Group and then led the European Bioscience Business Unit at COBA-Renaissance. In the 2000s, he led Datamonitor's Healthcare Division and founded two boutique management consultancies (NovaSecta, specializing in mid-sized pharmaceutical companies; and Unleash Team, focused on change management in scientific and technical organizations). He was a non-executive director on the board of Alpharma (an NYSE-listed mid-sized pharmaceutical corporation) from 2003 to 2006. Robert holds a Bachelor's degree in Mathematics from Imperial College London, and a Master's degree in Management from the Massachusetts Institute of Technology's Sloan School of Management. He publishes a regular blog and can be reached via the contact page on his website http://scitechstrategy.com.

List of Chapters

Contents

ACKNOWLEDGEMENTS

This book was over two years in the making and a lot of people contributed to its completion. Many individuals gave me the benefit of their thoughts and experiences, although I have anonymized many of the quotes in the text to protect the innocent. I would like to say a big thank you to each and every one of them.

My initial insights and hypotheses for this book stemmed from engaging with hundreds of executives, managers, project leaders, and scientists in the course of the consulting projects and industry networking initiatives that I had the privilege to lead. It would be impossible to list everyone who had influenced me, but in particular, much of the thinking behind this book was inspired, directly or indirectly, by the many creative, open-minded, and intense conversations I had with a few specific individuals: Sergio Cantoreggi and Giorgio Calderari at Helsinn; Reijo Salonen, Minna Ruotsalainen, Timo Lotta, and Tero Närvänen at Orion Pharma; Kjell-Erik Nordby, initially at Photocure and then at Weifa and Vistin Pharma; Tore Duvold, initially at LEO Pharma and then at Aker Biopharma; and former consulting colleagues Therese Sofie Kinal and Corrina Kane.

The specific content of this book was then developed and fine-tuned in a series of exploratory one-on-one interviews and small group workshops conducted between mid-2013 and early 2015. I am very much indebted to everyone who participated, and I would like to express my gratitude to (in alphabetical order of their organization at the time of our discussions):

- Edwin Moses, Tony de Fougerolles, Johan Heylen, Kim Simonsen, Holger Neecke, Pieter Schoen, Peter Meerts, Erik Depla, and Cedric Ververken of Ablynx.
- Murray Skinner of Allergy Therapeutics.
- Kemal Malik, Eckhard Ottow, Hans Lindner, Christoph Huwe, Holger Hess-Stumpp, Elke Dittrich-Wengenroth, Alexander Bertram, Daniel Forler, Joerg Knaeblein, Heidrun Dorsch, and Stefan Jaroch of Bayer HealthCare.
- Ken Rhodes, Tim Harris, and Jo Viney of Biogen Idec.
- Steven Gilman of Cubist Pharmaceuticals.
- Ruth Wellenreuther, Frank Westermann, Markus Feuerer, Stefan Pusch, and Caroline Weschke of the German Cancer Research Center (Deutsches Krebsforschungszentrum).
- Ivan Gergel of Endo Pharmaceuticals.
- Jan van de Winkel, Martine van Vugt, Janine Schuurman, Riemke van Dijkhuizen-Radersma, Erik Ensing, Frank Rebers, and Barbara Fiorini Due of Genmab.
- Fiona Marshall, Tim Tasker, Miles Congreve, Ali Jazayeri, and Rob Cooke of Heptares.
- Brian Cali and Todd Milne of Ironwood Pharmaceuticals.
- Roger Bone, Louise Jopling, and Ellen Rose of the Johnson & Johnson Innovation Center in London.
- Lars Klareskog and Louise Berg of the Karolinska Institutet.
- Bernhard Kirschbaum of Merck Serono.
- Simon Moroney of MorphoSys.
- Justin Bryans of MRC Technology.
- Per Falk, Lars Karlsson, Jerry Siu, and Peter Kurtzhals of Novo Nordisk.
- Reijo Salonen, Antti Haapalinna, Taru Blom, Timo Lotta, Minna Ruotsalainen, Eeva-Riitta Tammilehto, Jukka Sallinen, Pekka Kallio, Leena Otsomaa, Anu Moilanen, Ullamari Pesonen, David Din Belle, Harri Salo, Carina

Stenfors, Tim Holmström, Mika Mustonen, Juha Rouru, Lasse Kervinen, Leena Sopanen, and Mervi Niskanen of Orion Pharma.

- John Bell, Chas Bountra, Marc Feldmann, Maxine Allen, Oliver Voss, and Jutta Roth of the University of Oxford.
- John Dawson, Peter Nolan, Kyriacos Mitrophanous, James Miskin, Alex Lewis, and Kati Hudson of Oxford Biomedica.
- Janet White of Pfizer.
- John Burt and Jeff Edwards of Polytherics.
- Frank Grams, Andy Keesler, Jean-Paul Pasquet, Ekkehard Leberer, Marie-Noelle Castel, David Wang, and Varavani Dwarki of Sanofi.
- Pawel Przewiezlikowski and Mateusz Nowak of Selvita.
- Tom Large of Sunovion Pharmaceuticals.
- Ismail Kola of UCB Pharma.
- Mike Wood, Rod Hubbard, James Murray, and Ben Davis of Vernalis Research.
- Peter Mueller of Vertex Pharmaceuticals.

My thanks to Linda Allan of the University of Cambridge for encouraging me to test some of the ideas in this book with her students in the Master's in Bioscience Enterprise (MBE) program.

A big thank you also to my editor MaryAnne Gobble—she was simply brilliant at converting my convoluted prose into clearly articulated arguments and cleaning up the stylistic mess I had created in my initial draft!

Finally, this book would not have been possible without the unhesitating support of my family—my wife Marie, son Alasdair, and daughter Nathalie—whose faith and love encouraged me to pursue researching and writing this book while juggling the pressures of consultancy projects and the demands of family life.

List of Acronyms

ADME	Absorption, distribution, metabolism, excretion
API	Active pharmaceutical ingredient
ASAP	Association of Strategic Alliance Professionals
CD	Candidate drug
CDMO	Contract development & manufacturing organization
CMC	Chemical manufacturing and control
CMO	Contract manufacturing organization
COGS	Cost of goods
COPD	Chronic obstructive pulmonary disease
CRO	Contract research organization
ECQ	External collaborative quotient
EMA	European Medicines Agency
FDA	US Food and Drug Administration
FDF	Finished dosage form
FiM	First-in-man
GCP	Good Clinical Practice
GLP	Good Laboratory Practice
GMP	Good Manufacturing Practice
GPCR	G-protein coupled receptor
GSK	GlaxoSmithKline
IP	Intellectual property
J&J	Johnson & Johnson
JOC	Joint operating committee
JPT	Joint project team
JRC	Joint review committee
JSC	Joint steering committee
KOL	Key opinion leader

KPI	Key performance indicator
LCM	Life cycle management
MA	Marketing authorization
MRC	Medical Research Council
MRCT	MRC Technology
NDA	New drug application
NME	New molecular entity
NPV	Net present value
PI	Principal investigator
PoC	Proof-of-concept
ROI	Return on investment
SAB	Scientific advisory board
SME	Small to medium-sized enterprise

Chapter 1
Introduction and User Guide

The past decade has seen a massive shift in how new drugs and other therapies are discovered, developed, and commercialized. Large pharmaceutical companies, facing the end of many blockbuster drug patents and a dramatic decline in R&D productivity, needed to find new ways to power the next wave of innovation—the ground-breaking medicines that will keep them in business for another generation. This pressure has produced a new paradigm for biopharma R&D, one that seamlessly blends external partnerships with in-house research and development, resulting in an approach that is as likely to find the next blockbuster in the lab of a small startup or academic researcher as in internal work.

Smaller companies have been both beneficiaries and targets of this shift in focus. Working with a giant corporation can provide resources to develop and market inventions that small companies simply don't have, but it also brings unexpected challenges and new demands. And there are very few resources to help these "little guys" navigate these relationships—a gap this book intends to address.

This book is about R&D partnerships in **biopharma** R&D.[1] In particular, we focus on the most established form of these partnerships, namely the **bilateral partnership**—one involving two partners. Specifically, we look at **asymmetric partnerships**, David & Goliath arrangements in which one partner is a small organization (David) and one is a large company (Goliath). Although multilateral consortia and crowdsourcing have been the subject of much media attention recently, two-party relationships continue to be the most common kind of collaborations, and the large number of bilateral partnerships executed in the past has created a rich base of hard-won lessons, many of which can be applied with little or no adaptation to other forms of collaboration.

This book primarily adopts the David perspective, focusing on issues and challenges of concern to the smaller partner in such arrangements. Relatively few discussions to date have explicitly considered this perspective; furthermore, my recent consulting experience has primarily been in helping these smaller organizations navigate **David & Goliath partnerships**.

We start this introductory chapter by describing how the large multinational pharmaceutical companies (colloquially referred to as **big pharmas**) have transformed their R&D model, increasingly relying on externalization and shifting of their resources toward **bioclusters** (geographic regions with large concentrations of bioscience organizations), which offer a critical mass of potential partners. We go on to highlight the proliferation of David & Goliath partnerships as a major theme in the emergence of the new biopharma R&D paradigm. Next, we explain more fully the scope, target audience, and origin of this book. And finally, to close this chapter, we provide a high-level overview of the book's contents and offer some suggestions on how best to use it.

The Transformation of Big Pharma R&D

The big pharmas have dramatically overhauled their R&D models over the past ten to fifteen years in response to a relentless industrywide decline in R&D productivity (the root causes of which are discussed in Chapter 2). The key theme of this shift has been R&D externalization—looking outside the company's in-house labs for the next big breakthroughs. Most big pharmas now operate a mixed R&D model, seeking external partners and accessing ideas for development from other organizations while continuing to conduct a proportion of R&D projects in-house, both to hedge their bets and to maintain the know-how to select and work with the best external ideas, technologies, and partners. However, some industry commentators have gone so far as to postulate that it might make economic sense for some companies to completely outsource earlier-stage research.[2]

This is abundantly evident in the therapies now in the pipeline. Of a list of thirty of the world's most promising prospective new drugs for 2014—including ten that "could transform the industry with game-changing commercial potential" and twenty others of "potentially high impact"—venture capitalist Bruce Booth noted that only eight had originated in-house; fourteen were in-licensed and the remaining eight came from acquisitions.[3] An analysis of the inventors of 252 new drugs approved by the US Food and Drug Administration (FDA) from 1998 to 2007 concluded that drugs initially discovered in biotechnology companies or universities accounted for 56% of the scientifically innovative drugs approved, as well as 53% of those that responded to unmet medical needs.[4] Another study reported that the share of pharmaceutical R&D projects directly managed by small organizations (defined in the study as those having fewer than fourteen active R&D projects) had doubled between the 1990–1999 and 2000–2007 periods.[5] In contrast, the total number of FDA-approved new molecular entities (NMEs) that were initially discovered in the labs of the big pharmas fell from 75% in the 1980s to just 35% in 2007.[6]

The trend is also evident in scholarly productivity; a recent analysis of top-tier academic publications in the pharmaceutical R&D domain demonstrated a clear decline over the past decade in the number of lead authors working for big pharma corporations and highlighted the widening number of different organizations involved in each research paper (Figure 1.1).[7]

***Figure 1.1.* A Bibliometric Perspective on Big Pharma's R&D Decline**

	1998	2009
Average number of organizations represented per article	2.1	3.6
Collaborative articles as proportion of total	62%	72%
Of these collaborative publications:		
Proportion with big pharma–based first author	43%	35%
Proportion with big pharma–based corresponding author	41%	34%

Source: Data from Rafols et al., "Big Pharma, Little Science?" (2014), who report on a study of 2,000 publications per year of analysis, randomly extracted from the 200 top pharmaceuticals journals.

Those projects are delivering real value. According to an industry study by consultancy firm Deloitte, in 2014, an average of 58% of the value of late-stage new product pipelines across a cohort of twelve of the largest big pharmas were sourced externally (Figure 1.2).[8] The proportions for individual companies ranged from 35% to 85%, with three-quarters of the companies exhibiting over 50% externalization. This was not a new development; 2014 was the fifth consecutive year of the Deloitte study in which external sources comprised the majority of late-stage pipeline value. In 2014, half of these externally sourced late-stage projects represented licensing or co-development collaborations. And of the remaining half that came from corporate acquisitions, a good number had started as successful collaborations between the acquirer and the acquired.

***Figure 1.2.* Average Contribution to Value by Asset Source: Late-Stage Pipelines of 12 Largest Big Pharma Companies**

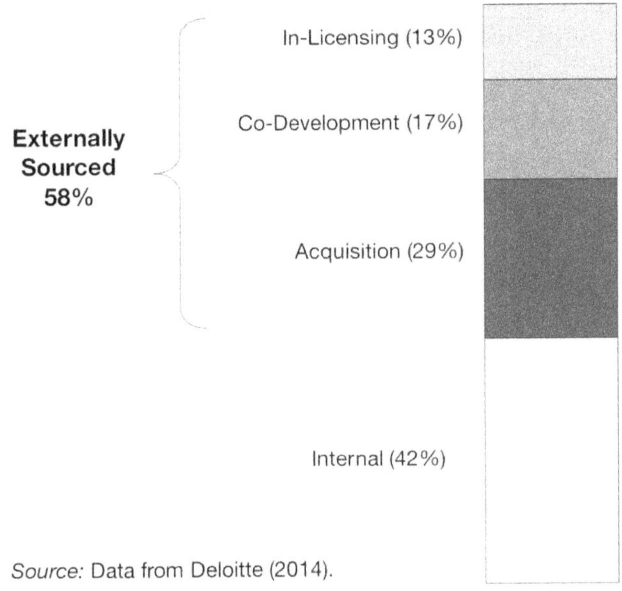

Source: Data from Deloitte (2014).

The Deloitte study noted that the mean risk-adjusted peak sales of prospective drugs in its sample was higher for externally sourced projects by 6% for all projects, by 20% for "breakthrough therapy" drugs, and by 54% for drugs with an orphan designation (that is, those developed to treat very rare diseases). Hence, externally sourced projects are on average more valuable than internally generated ones, especially for those intended to address challenging medical needs for which healthcare payers are open to higher prices.

The same study also noted that, on average, assets sourced at an earlier stage subsequently performed better in late-stage clinical trials and in the marketplace. This finding initially seems counterintuitive—later-stage projects are closer to the marketplace and in theory should come with less risk. However, it appears that the earlier input of regulatory and commercial expertise from the eventual marketer of the drug increases the chances of successful later-stage approval and reimbursement. Furthermore, deals made at a later stage carry a hefty price premium, depressing the return on investment (ROI) for the eventual marketer. In addition to partnering projects, there continues to be steady growth in the outsourcing of particular R&D operations to **contract research organizations** (CROs). According to a market research report published by Business Wire in 2015, the clinical trial outsourcing market is expected to grow at a compound rate of 9% per year between 2015 and 2020, leading to an astounding rate of clinical trial outsourcing—by 2020, 72% of all clinical trials will be outsourced.[9]

At the same time that companies are dispersing R&D to external partners, biopharma R&D has increasingly consolidated geographically, coalescing around fast-growing geographic bioclusters that provide hubs for bioscience research and innovation. Each biocluster typically comprises important academic research institutions with deep strengths in the medical and bioscience arenas; major research and teaching hospitals; and large numbers of smaller biotech, medical technology, CRO, and other service and **technology provider** companies, creating a bioscience innovation ecosystem. Some of the more prominent and established bioclusters include:

- In the United States, greater Boston, Massachusetts; the San Francisco Bay area and greater San Diego in California; and the Research Triangle Park in North Carolina.
- In the United Kingdom, the Cambridge-London-Oxford Golden Triangle and Edinburgh, Scotland.
- In Germany, Berlin and Munich.
- In Paris, the area south of Paris, between Paris-Saclay and Genopole.
- The BioValley, an area which spans Switzerland, southwestern Germany, and French Alsace.

- The Medicon Valley, a region comprising Copenhagen in Denmark and Malmo and Lund, both in Sweden.
- In China, greater Shanghai.

Many others are emerging and expanding in Europe, North America, and Asia.

As the big pharmas have trimmed and streamlined their traditional, monolithic R&D sites, they are building smaller, more nimble units in these bioclusters. For example, GlaxoSmithKline (GSK) closed its long-established research center in Verona (Italy) and greatly expanded its research center in Shanghai. Pfizer closed its site in Sandwich (UK) and scaled down its site in Groton, Connecticut (US), while setting up new research units in Boston/Cambridge, Massachusetts (US), and Cambridge (UK). AstraZeneca is closing its R&D center at Alderley Park (UK) and building a new R&D center in Cambridge (UK). And the list goes on.

This geographic refocusing of R&D activities by the big pharmas has had the paradoxical effect of strengthening and expanding the smaller bioscience companies and academic research groups. While the widely publicized site closures and layoffs associated with the shutdown of big R&D centers have had a significant human cost, there has also been a redistribution of talent and infrastructure to smaller companies, CROs, and academic research labs. For example, when Pfizer decided to close its R&D center at Sandwich in 2011, the site employed 2,400 people on a 340-acre campus. By mid-2015, that same site had morphed into Discovery Park, a science and technology park that hosted over 100 companies employing more people than Pfizer had at that location. A similar story is emerging at AstraZeneca's center at Alderley Park. Hence, in addition to partnering more with David, Goliath is also fueling an expansion of the number of Davids and strengthening their capabilities through its restructuring activities.

Thus, driven by economic and scientific imperatives, the principles of the global open innovation movement[10] are starting to take hold in the biopharma sector. The new biopharma R&D paradigm is now highly collaborative and externalized, and the language of partnering is part of everyday vocabulary in the industry (see "Partnering Speak," below). Participation in multilateral consortia is accelerating. Crowdsourcing of technical solutions and innovative ideas is starting to become an element in the R&D mix for an increasing number of the big pharmas. And bilateral partnerships—particularly with small, innovative companies and academic researchers—are now an established way of doing business at all stages of the R&D value chain.

Big pharmas concentrate the bulk of their in-house resources on later-stage development and commercialization while sourcing ideas, technologies, and a large proportion of their earlier-stage projects from smaller bioscience firms and academic research groups. A rapidly expanding global CRO sector provides specialized services to both large and small players. And all these actors are focusing their activities around an increasing number of fast-growing geographic bioscience clusters.

Partnering Speak

In the world of collaborative biopharma R&D, there are some colloquial terms that can have ambiguous or multiple interpretations. For the sake of clarity, we define here how such words and phrases are used in this book.

When we refer to a **collaboration**, we mean a set of activities with planned outcomes and timelines in which two or more organizationally separate parties work with each other to achieve a mutual benefit; that set of activities is structured as a **collaborative project**. We will also use *project* interchangeably with *collaboration* when it is clear what we mean in context.

Partnership, or its synonym **alliance**, refers both to the collaboration and to the arrangements between the parties in a collaboration to allocate and share resources, operating responsibilities, decision making, benefits, and risks, regardless of whether such arrangements have been set out in a formal contract. Depending on the context, the partnership (or alliance) may encompass a single collaboration (or project) or a group of related collaborations (or projects). Occasionally, we will refer to a **deal** to mean the joint decision between the parties to go ahead with a partnership.

Collaboration management, or its synonym **alliance management**, denotes those activities carried out to ensure that partnerships proceed to their goals efficiently, effectively, and harmoniously. Specifying these two phrases as equivalent is somewhat at odds with the way we define *collaboration* and *alliance* above, but it reflects common usage.

Alliance managers are people who carry out alliance management activities, whether in a dedicated role or as part of other duties or whether they have this or some other job title. Many organizations have dedicated **corporate alliance management groups** or functions that provide an organizational home for alliance managers and also conduct other activities beyond the scope of individual alliance managers, such as managing a portfolio of alliances.

Defining the David & Goliath Partnership

As a result of the changes in biopharma R&D approaches, many small organizations are finding themselves in asymmetric, bilateral R&D partnerships—David & Goliath arrangements in which the two parties are mismatched not just in size but also in strategic business aims, operating models, organizational cultures, and relative power. These arrangements may be **product innovation partnerships**, in which both parties share ownership in the outcome, or **value-added outsourcing partnerships**, in which a project sponsor contracts with a provider of customized services or IP-protected technology. These relationships bring new opportunities to small companies, but they also bring significant new challenges. This book explores those challenges and offers advice for navigating them, to ensure successful outcomes for both parties.

The vast majority of biopartnering articles, conferences, and networking events emphasize the deal-making end of the partnering process, focusing on finding, designing, and structuring such partnerships. But what really matters in the long run is whether partnerships deliver innovations that both improve the health of the world and provide an adequate return on investment to all the collaborating parties—here, there is still huge room for improvement. Consequently, in this book, we adopt a **benefit delivery perspective**, focusing on those factors, besides the obvious scientific elements, that influence the emergence of valuable outputs from such partnerships.

In my experience, people from the David side of asymmetric R&D partnerships struggle the most to understand and cope with what they perceive as difficult behaviors and illogical decisions from their Goliath counterparts. So my primary audience for this book is those in David organizations who are (or plan to be) participants in partnerships with multinational Goliath corporations—including senior executives, scientific line managers, project leaders, alliance managers, and bench scientists from smaller companies, as well as industry liaison managers, principal investigators, alliance managers, postdocs, and PhD students from academia. Hopefully, this book can provide a helpful reference as you live through the different stages of your partnerships.

The book should also be of interest to those in Goliath organizations who are regularly involved in R&D partnerships with smaller partners—including project leaders, alliance managers, scientific line managers, and bench scientists working in the partnerships day to day, as well as senior executives serving on governance committees. Business development executives and managers from both David and Goliath organizations would benefit from a better understanding of benefit-delivery issues and how the choices made at the outset of partnerships can influence outcomes far down the line. And last but not least, students in graduate courses in business or the biosciences should find this book a useful overview of the key topics and issues in biopharma R&D partnering.

For those who have participated in many David & Goliath R&D collaborations, there should not be many surprises in this book. My aim for this experienced group is to provide a better appreciation of the extent to which their own experiences are prevalent across the industry and help them reflect on and learn from those experiences. For those who are less experienced, I aim to help you understand why some things are the way they are, anticipate important issues and opportunities, avoid some common pitfalls, and in general improve the chances of successful outcomes from your partnerships.

Having said that, I am not providing a detailed cookbook; there are no step-by-step recipes for building a successful partnership. The world of biopharma R&D is simply too complex and unpredictable to manage in such a cookie-cutter fashion. At the end of the day, R&D partnerships are about people working together. Given the diversity of humankind and the complexity and relative immaturity of the biological sciences, there are no hard and fast templates for executing a successful biopharma R&D collaboration. The right answer to any given dilemma will always depend on the particular situation at hand and the specific people involved.

This book articulates what I believe, based on my research and substantial experience in the field, are the important things to get right and the pitfalls to avoid. It draws specifically upon my experiences and perspectives developed working with more than forty different biopharma organizations (see "Origin of this Book," below). In half of these cases, I have had the privilege of working closely with the relevant organization on important initiatives or projects. For the remainder, I conducted interviews and small group workshops specifically for this book. I do not claim to have undertaken a rigorous scientific study; my viewpoints and conclusions derive from my own empirical synthesis of what I have seen and heard, subjectively interpreted through the filter of nearly twenty-five years' experience in the biopharma sector.

Origin of this Book

The starting hypotheses for this book grew from my personal reflections on a decade of working closely with senior executives and scientific leaders at twenty small and medium-sized enterprises (SMEs) in the biopharma, medical technology, and contract research sectors across a dozen countries. Most of these organizations were European, with a smattering in the United States and China.

I developed my thinking further by conducting my own primary research, including individual interviews and small group workshops at more than twenty additional biopharma, medical technology, and academic organizations. Again, most of this research was conducted in Europe, with a small number of participating organizations in the United States. I started with an initial round of twenty open-ended face-to-face interviews conducted in summer 2013 and spring 2014. These interviews helped shape my ideas and focus the key concepts, leading me to publish a number of articles on my blog in the autumn of 2014. To validate and further enrich the discussion, I embarked on a second round of in-depth workshops and focus interviews with a dozen biopharma and academic organizations, half of whom I had neither interviewed nor worked with historically; these discussions took place between autumn 2014 and spring 2015.

In total, this book draws on the partnering experiences and perspectives of more than forty different organizations, of which approximately 20% have been involved in partnerships in a Goliath role, 50% in a David role, and 30% in both Goliath and David roles.

A User Guide for this Book

This book is made up of twelve chapters—this introductory chapter and eleven other chapters that map the distinctive characteristics of biopharma R&D; describe the benefits, risks, and challenges of partnering; and lay out practical considerations and important trends in biopharma R&D partnering. We have listed acronyms used at the front of the book. We have also compiled a comprehensive glossary at the back of the book; the first use in the text of a glossary term is highlighted in **bold**.

Part A: Foundations

2. The Characteristics of Biopharma R&D
3. The Benefits and Risks of Partnering
4. Bilateral R&D Partnership Models
5. Archetypes of Collaborating Organizations

Part A introduces the key concepts governing biopharma partnering, and especially bilateral partnerships, and provides a framework for understanding these partnerships.

Chapter 2 chronicles the industrywide decline in R&D productivity that led to the emergence of the new biopharma R&D paradigm we see today and goes into some detail with regard to the peculiarities that affect the dynamics of biopharma R&D projects and determine the value inflection points in the life cycle of such projects. Experienced industry insiders or those who are very familiar with the project dynamics of biopharma R&D may safely skip this chapter; those whose experience base is in academic research, business development, or the commercial arena will hopefully find the discussion illuminating.

Chapter 3 discusses the benefits and risks of working collaboratively and introduces the important notions of execution risk, collaboration risk, and the collaboration tax. We discuss the implications of these concepts and explain the financial mechanisms typically used to share risk and return in bilateral R&D partnerships.

Chapter 4 provides a framework and terminology for characterizing the different types of bilateral partnerships that are frequently observed in practice. We illustrate the diversity of approaches that have been implemented, highlight the distinctive features of these models, provide a useful shorthand for later use in the book, and highlight some key dos and don'ts.

Finally, Chapter 5 describes the most commonly encountered collaborating organizations in biopharma R&D partnerships, categorizing them as archetypes. For each archetype, we look at the strategic aims and business models that drive these organizations, their rationale for R&D partnerships, their key stakeholders and internal processes, and the values, culture, and other drivers that influence their behavior in R&D partnerships.

Part B: Improving the Odds

6. Partnership Strategy and Design
7. Setting Up the Project Structure
8. Navigating Partnership Execution
9. Leveraging Alliance Managers

Part B dives into the practical aspects of David & Goliath R&D partnerships, looking at what can be done at the different stages of a partnership to improve the odds of beneficial outcomes, for the participating parties and for healthcare in general. Over these four chapters, we walk through the life cycle of a partnership to discuss the key issues and opportunities at each stage.

Chapter 6 considers how organizations triage prospective partnerships in the context of an overall partnering strategy. It then looks at how partnerships are designed and negotiated and points out some common misconceptions and blind spots in the due diligence process that follows partnership negotiation and precedes final execution of a deal.

Chapter 7 discusses the important considerations in designing the project structure—how the project will be organized, conducted, and governed, and most importantly by whom. This is a key activity in the transition period between the signing of the deal and the commencement of operations. We look especially at the people aspects of the project, including the choice of which individuals will participate and in what roles, their attributes and motivations, their expectations for how the partnership journey will go, and the mindset they adopt when they engage with each other.

Chapter 8 concentrates on the execution phase of the collaboration, beginning with a close look at the honeymoon period at the outset of a partnership. We then discuss the issues associated with the inevitable stage transitions during execution. We conclude the chapter by looking at the periodic maintenance actions that are helpful for ensuring a partnership continues to run smoothly.

We conclude Part B with Chapter 9, which delves into the important role alliance managers play in David & Goliath partnerships. We look at the work of alliance managers in detail, first highlighting the processes they look after and the tools they deploy and then describing some of the problematic situations they are called upon to resolve. We conclude the chapter by discussing what makes a good alliance manager.

Part C: Trends Looking Forward

10. Trends in Big Pharma Partnering
11. The Rise of Nonprofit R&D: Case Studies in Drug Discovery
12. Emergence of the Networked R&D Organization

Over the final three chapters of the book, we highlight some important trends with respect to collaboration in the biopharma

R&D ecosystem. Although our primary context is bilateral R&D partnerships, these trends are also relevant to multilateral consortia and other new forms of collaboration inspired by the open innovation movement.

Chapter 10 looks at the efforts of some large, multinational companies to upgrade partnering-related functions over the past few years. Having recognized that partnerships are now part of their daily business, these companies have sought to establish significant corporate alliance management functions, institutionalize alliance management processes and tools, and reshape the paradigm of innovation scouting from deal sourcing to relationship building and networking.

Chapter 11 looks at the increasing role played by academia and nonprofit organizations in biopharma R&D. We illustrate this developing trend by describing two models increasingly being adopted in the drug discovery domain, namely industry-academic co-discovery alliances and nonprofit drug discovery organizations.

Finally, in Chapter 12, we look at how a growing number of organizations are becoming networked R&D organizations that excel at partnering. We consider how organizations evolve as they seek to get better at partnering, a journey that leads down one of two paths, resulting in an organization that is either partnering-savvy or partnering-centric.

Being David

As big pharmas have come to grips with the precipitous decline in their R&D productivity, they have embraced a new, distributed R&D model, one that relies on collaborations and acquisitions as much as in-house research to generate innovation and create value. Often, they turn to small, innovative companies and academic researchers for new ideas and leading-edge scientific expertise. This trend presents new opportunities for academic labs and SMEs—but it also presents significant challenges. If these asymmetric collaborations are to deliver value for both sides, the Davids in these David & Goliath partnerships must come to grips with Goliath's perspective and develop the practices and mindset to face these challenges head-on. It is the goal of this book to help Davids achieve this aim.

Chapter Notes

[1] Over the past two decades, there has been a blurring of lines between traditional pharmaceutical corporations and newer biotechnology companies. In this book, we define the biopharma sector as the domain of activity related to researching, innovating, developing, and commercializing new or improved disease therapies, regardless of whether these arise from traditional small molecule drugs, the more complex biologic drugs, or emerging new approaches such as gene therapy.

[2] See, for example, A. Baum et al., *Pharmaceuticals: Exit Research and Create Value,* Morgan Stanley Research, January 20, 2010.

[3] Bruce Booth, "Transformational Late-Stage Drugs Delivered Through Deal-Making," *Forbes*, March 21, 2014, http://www.forbes.com/sites/brucebooth/2014/03/21/transformational-late-stage-drugs-delivered-through-deal-making/.

[4] See Thomas Sullivan, "The Importance of Companies for Pharmaceutical Discovery: Origins of a Decade of New Products," *Policy and Medicine,* November 10, 2010, http://www.policymed.com/2010/11/the-importance-of-companies-for-pharmaceutical-discovery-origins-of-a-decade-of-new-products.html.

[5] F. Pammolli, L. Magazzini, and M. Riccaboni, "The Productivity Crisis in Pharmaceutical R&D," *Nature Reviews Drug Discovery* 10 (June 2011): 428–438.

[6] B. Munos, "Lessons from 60 Years of Pharmaceutical Innovation," *Nature Reviews Drug Discovery* 8 (December 2009): 959–968.

[7] I. Rafols, M. Hopkins, J. Hoekman, J. Siepel, A. O'Hare, A. Perianes-Rodríguez, and P. Nightingale, "Big Pharma, Little Science? A Bibliometric Perspective on Big Pharma's R&D Decline," *Technological Forecasting & Social Change* 81 (January 2014): 22–38.

[8] Deloitte, *Measuring the Return from Pharmaceutical Innovation 2014: Turning a Corner?*, Deloitte Centre for Health Solutions, 2014. The cohort for this ongoing study, which has remained consistent since 2010, comprises the top twelve publicly listed, research-based life science companies in terms of 2008–2009 R&D spending. This list comprises Amgen, AstraZeneca, Bristol-Myers Squibb, Eli Lilly, GlaxoSmithKline, Johnson & Johnson, Merck & Co., Novartis, Pfizer, Roche, Sanofi, and Takeda.

[9] *Business Wire*, "Research and Markets: The New 2015 Trends of Global Clinical Development Outsourcing Market," January 30, 2015, http://www.businesswire.com/news/home/20150130005621/en/Research-Markets-2015-Trends-Global-Clinical-Development.

[10] See Henry Chesbrough, *Open Innovation: The New Imperative for Creating and Profiting from Technology* (Boston, MA: Harvard Business School Press, 2003).

Part A: Foundations

Part A introduces key concepts and provides a framework for understanding bilateral R&D partnerships and particularly David & Goliath partnerships.

CHAPTER 2
THE CHARACTERISTICS OF BIOPHARMA R&D

The shift in the biopharma industry, from massive in-house R&D to a distributed, networked model that relies on partnerships and acquisitions, has emerged in reaction to a long-term decline in the productivity of big pharma R&D efforts. That decline is driven by a wide range of factors. Biopharma R&D has always been characterized by complexity, long life cycles, and high risk. External forces, such as changes in the economics of healthcare and increasing regulatory pressures, have combined with a tendency toward both scientific and management reductionism to accentuate the difficulties of biopharma R&D. Taken together, these challenges have forced big pharma to reconsider how it pursues innovation and generates value, creating opportunities for smaller, more agile organizations.

In this chapter, we discuss the characteristics of biopharma R&D that distinguish it from R&D in other industries, including the many complexities related to **biological pathways** and **drug targets**, challenging regulator and payer hurdles, and very long project durations. These peculiarities, which lead to high costs, multiple value inflection points, low probabilities of success, and convoluted project paths with high unpredictability, have driven an industrywide decline in biopharma R&D productivity over the past sixty years, one that is only now beginning to reverse itself as big pharma companies adopt new models for their R&D efforts.

The Unique Dynamics of Biopharma R&D

Biopharma R&D is distinguished from other industries in several respects, all springing from the peculiar nature of the pharmaceutical industry. Scientific complexity and high regulatory and economic hurdles for approval and market access lead to projects of very long duration (Figure 2.1), with high costs and very low chances of success. The full process of developing a drug, from starting the discovery effort to making the drug available on the market, could take as long as fifteen to twenty years. Once a particular biological pathway has been prioritized, it could take three to six years, or even longer, to validate a drug target on that pathway and then test thousands of new molecule variants to identify a **candidate drug** (CD) for that target. The subsequent development of that candidate over a program of *in vitro, in vivo,* and clinical studies could take a further eight to twelve years. Even after the first regulatory approval in a major market, it can take another one to three years to gain access to all the major global markets.

Figure 2.1. **Biopharma R&D Project Life Cycle**

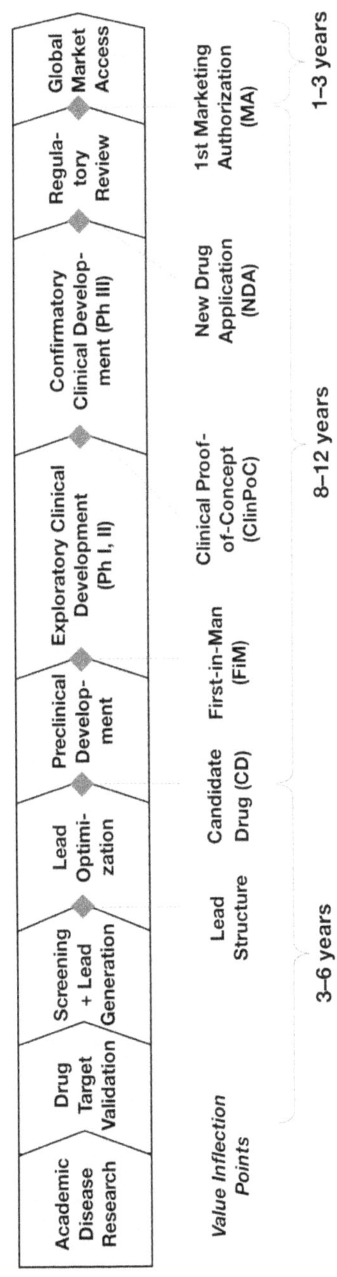

That long duration has a number of implications for the R&D effort. Circumstances can change dramatically even as companies are investing in a project. New scientific evidence can modify or invalidate the project's original hypothesis. New technological tools can open up unanticipated opportunities. Regulator hurdles and payer priorities can change. The people involved, and their priorities and aspirations for the project, can also change, both because of natural organizational attrition and because the project requires different skill sets at different phases of its life cycle. And organizational ownership of the project can often change, as well, typically moving from an academic or SME lab to a big pharma with the resources to fund the huge costs of late-stage clinical development and gain worldwide market access.

All of this means that a project's path to market is not straightforward or predictable. Unlike, for instance, a typical information technology or aerospace R&D effort, customer requirements cannot be matched with technological feasibility to specify precise product characteristics that can be engineered into the resulting product. In biopharma R&D, it is not sufficient to define a project plan incorporating mostly predictable tasks and then manage the project for adherence to timelines and budgets. Rather, the project journey is a long and windy road, involving a large number of unknowns leading to beneficial detours and hopeless dead ends as market conditions and scientific knowledge evolve over the project duration, with serendipity playing no small part in the final outcome.

That unpredictable journey means that a project also has several value inflection points, moments at which the market value of the project—the amount another organization would be willing to pay for it on the open market—changes dramatically, disproportionately to the total investment made in the project thus far. The scale of the change at one of the value inflection point (whether positive or negative) can be large enough to have a dramatic effect on the enterprise value of the project's parent organization. There are four critical inflection points for drugs based on innovative NMEs:

- ***Candidate drug (CD).*** At least one patented candidate drug has been generated and is ready to start the regulator-mandated program of formal *in vivo* safety studies that is the precursor to the FiM inflection point.
- ***First-in-man (FiM).*** The first human clinical trial of the CD has been initiated.
- ***Clinical proof-of-concept (PoC or ClinPoC).*** Data indicating strong evidence of **efficacy** has been generated in comparatively small Phase II clinical trials with idealized patient samples combined with acceptable absorption, distribution, metabolism, excretion (ADME) and toxicology data from human and animal trials.
- ***Marketing authorization (MA).*** Drug has been approved for marketing; product license granted by the regulatory authority in at least one major geographic market.

Increasingly, another significant value inflection point is the achievement of market access through agreement on a commercially viable pricing scheme with key healthcare payers in a major geographic market. This is especially the case if the new drug replaces low-cost generic drugs as the commonly accepted treatment for a particular indication.

There are a few other inflection points that could have a major impact on a project's value in specific circumstances:

- ***Lead structure/series.*** A patentable series of molecules has been discovered from which one or more candidate drugs can be derived. This is especially significant if the drug target concerned is **precedented** (that is, other organizations have had attractive clinical trial results on this target with other candidate drugs) and the data on the new series of molecules suggests a viable source of competitive differentiation.

- *New drug application (NDA).* The full NDA documentation package has been filed with a recognized regulatory authority.
- *Additional marketing authorization.* The drug has won marketing authorization from a regulatory agency in another geographic market, especially a major one such as the United States, the European Union, or Japan.
- *Line extension.* The drug has won approval for another indication, especially one that greatly expands the drug's potential market size.
- *Life cycle management (LCM) approval.* The drug's period of exclusivity has been extended by gaining approval for a patented variant of the original drug that offers documented performance improvement over the original.

Given the long durations and complex evolutions, it should come as no surprise that biopharma projects are both very costly and very risky. According to a 2014 study by the Tufts Center for the Study of Drug Development, the average out-of-pocket expenditure to take a new drug from discovery to regulatory approval is US$1.4 billion; that number does not include an estimated US$1.2 billion in investment returns foregone.[1]

All of that money buys a very low probability of success. In the 2005–2010 period, the industry median success rate for bringing candidate drugs to market was only 6%, and some major companies fared even worse; the corresponding figure for AstraZeneca was only 2%.[2] And these statistics do not include the efforts to generate the candidate drugs in the first place or the post-approval efforts to gain market access at prices that can both cover the investments in successful projects and recoup the losses on the failed projects.

However, project success is relative to how a project's goals are defined. Many projects are deemed failures and canceled because they don't reach their original goals, but a candidate drug that fails for a particular **indication**, **label**, and patient population might well be viable for a different indication with a different label in a different patient population. The popularity of drug **repurposing**, in which another company makes a success of a candidate drug abandoned or sold by its original owner by applying it to a different indication or population or both, is evidence that a certain number of project teams or sponsors are myopic, unable to see opportunities beyond the original goals.

The Decline of Biopharma R&D Productivity

Over the past several decades, a number of forces have come together to exacerbate these challenges and reduce the productivity of big pharma's investment in R&D. Aggregate R&D productivity across the pharmaceutical industry fell steadily from 1950 to 2010. The extent of that decline is staggering; an often-quoted paper by Jack Scannell and his Sanford C. Bernstein colleagues estimates that the number of new approved drugs per billion inflation-adjusted US dollars spent on R&D has fallen eighty-fold since 1950, in effect halving every nine years.[3] Scannell and his team coined the term "Eroom's Law"—reversing Moore's Law, which describes the exponential increase in computing power over time in the information technology sector—to characterize the phenomenon.

This steady and rapid decline is even more dramatic in light of the huge advances that have come in that same period, both in the scientific understanding of disease and in R&D-enabling technologies such as combinatorial chemistry, high-throughput compound screening, genomic sequencing, and three-dimensional protein structure mapping, to name a few. But these technological advances have not accelerated R&D, as they have in other industries; rather, the productivity trend in pharmaceutical R&D has been worsening, a phenomenon that has inspired numerous studies by management academics as well as a plethora of articles by industry executives and consultants. The key findings from this literature identify four primary root causes of the productivity decline, namely:

- Health economics pressures.
- Increasing regulatory hurdles.
- Management reductionism and diseconomies of scale.
- Molecular reductionism.

These four elements are working together to put ever-increasing pressure on biopharma R&D.

Health Economics Pressures and Regulatory Hurdles

Researchers have observed a connection between decreasing R&D productivity and shifts in healthcare economics. In a 2011 study, Fabio Pammolli and his colleagues at the IMT Institute analyzed R&D productivity in terms of attrition rates, development times, and the number of NMEs launched.[4] They concluded that the sharp decline correlated strongly with an increased focus on unmet medical needs and altogether new treatment approaches—that is, projects with very low probabilities of success. This move, Pammolli and his colleagues note, was driven by the reimbursement practices of healthcare payers:

> Both private and public payers discourage incremental innovation and investments in follow-on drugs in already established therapeutic classes, mostly by the use of reference pricing schemes and bids designed to maximize the intensity of price competition among different molecules. Indeed, in established markets, innovative patented drugs are often reimbursed at the same level as older drugs.[5]

Scannell and his co-authors identify the same issue, which they entertainingly refer to as the "better than the Beatles" problem:

> Imagine how hard it would be to achieve commercial success with new pop songs if any new song had to be better than the Beatles, if the entire Beatles catalogue was available for free, and if people did not get bored with old Beatles records ... Yesterday's blockbuster is today's generic. An ever-improving back catalogue of approved medicines increases the complexity of the development process for new drugs.[6]

In other words, as continuing increases in lifespan and quality of life expectations brought about by improving healthcare put immense pressure on the budgets of healthcare payers, those payers in turn pressured pharmaceutical companies by reducing payouts and requiring patients to use generic alternatives. Healthcare payers are now primarily concerned about cost-effectiveness when considering a new drug. This means that in order to justify a higher level of reimbursement, the new drug must substantially outperform currently available generic drugs with regard to impact on total patient treatment costs, including hospitalization and post-discharge care.

Gaining market access for a new drug means getting healthcare payers to agree that most (if not all) of the drug's cost will be reimbursed. Without a significant **reimbursement level**, patients must bear a high proportion of the drug cost, severely constraining the potential market size in most cases. In order to achieve a favorable reimbursement decision, the pharmaceutical company and healthcare payer must agree on a mutually acceptable price or (as is increasingly the case with new innovative drugs) a contingent pricing structure such as a **pay-for-performance** arrangement in which retrospective bonuses or penalties are paid or assessed based on the health outcomes actually achieved in the patient population.

This trend is ongoing, continually magnifying the height of the performance mountain new drugs must climb to surmount the ever-growing back catalogue of cheap, generic drugs. As a result, biopharma companies have moved to prioritize tougher medical challenges with inherently lower probabilities of success. In other words, companies are deliberately choosing to invest in riskier efforts in a bid to achieve the higher prices and volumes promised by less intense competition and higher reimbursement rates, which can provide an adequate return on the R&D investment. In this way, health economics pressures push biopharma companies to experiment with new technologies and innovative treatment approaches.

But these new technologies and innovative treatments bring many unknowns—and with them, new risks. This reality, in turn, increases public concerns about safety and encourages regulators to increase the hurdles to market authorization, in terms of data requirements, statistical sample sizes, and patient group specificity. Increasing public distrust of the pharmaceutical industry has resulted in increasingly higher hurdles for efficacy, safety, and quality, as Scannell and colleagues note:

> Each real or perceived sin by the industry, or genuine drug misfortune, leads to a tightening of the regulatory ratchet, and the ratchet is rarely loosened, even if it seems as though this could be achieved without causing significant risk to drug safety.[7]

Before a new prescription drug can be used by physicians, it must clear three specific hurdles:

- *Efficacy*. The drug must have an observable impact on the disease symptoms or disease state progression, as measured by disease-specific metrics captured in clinical trials.
- *Safety*. The side effects of the drug must be medically acceptable at the normally prescribed dosage, as measured first in animal studies and subsequently in human clinical

trials. There is no absolute standard; rather, the level of acceptable side effects relates to the severity of the disease—what might be unacceptable for summer hay fever relief might be acceptable for a cancer patient with a high mortality risk.

- *Quality*. Each physical drug product must have the exact same composition of active pharmaceutical ingredients (APIs), inactive **excipients** (required to create the physical **finished dosage form** [FDF] administered to patients), and impurities as was tested in the clinical trials. For a new drug to be approved, its manufacturing process (including product testing procedures and production facilities) must also be approved. The manufacturing process cannot be altered without an application to the regulator that includes appropriate data to support the need to vary the process. The manufacturing process is subject to periodic inspection after the drug goes on the market, and a substandard performance on an inspection, even long after the initial market launch, could lead to regulatory approval being suspended or withdrawn.

Regulators approve a drug for use according to a defined dosing regimen with respect to a certain indication—a valid medical reason for use based on a particular set of physician-observed symptoms or diagnostic test results that characterize the patient's condition or disease severity. For each approved indication, acceptable usage is defined by three criteria:

- Whether the patient is part of the subpopulation for whom the drug is approved, as defined by a number of factors, including for example age, gender, the absence of certain **contraindications** (circumstances under which the drug should not be used, such as the presence of a concomitant disease or an allergy), or the presence of a specific **disease variant** as determined by a specific testable biomarker.

- Whether the drug can be prescribed as the initial therapy on first diagnosis—as a **first-line treatment**—or only as a recourse in case another treatment does not work—a **second-line treatment**.
- Whether the drug will be taken in combination with another drug or on its own.

All these elements—the indication, contraindications, and other treatment characteristics—constitute what is commonly referred to as the drug's label. A drug can be approved for multiple indications, each with its own label. The label defines what the pharmaceutical company is legally allowed to promote in terms of the drug's usage and relevant patient subpopulation; as such, from a commercial perspective, it essentially defines the size of the new drug's potential market. Physicians can prescribe a drug for an **off-label use** as long as they can medically justify that decision, but pharmaceutical companies cannot promote such off-label use; many have been fined heavily for attempting to do so. Hence, pharmaceutical companies typically seek to get a new drug approved for as many indications as possible, each with the widest possible label, in order to maximize the commercial return on the drug.

The approval process is further complicated by the need to seek approval separately in each country where the drug will be available, except in European Union countries, where a centralized approval path is an option. Each national regulatory agency has its own information requirements and decision criteria. In practice much (but not all) of the documentation required is fairly standardized, since most agencies have adopted standards similar to those employed by the United States Food and Drug Administration (FDA) or the European Medicines Agency (EMA). Nevertheless, each agency makes its own decision and the resulting approved indications and their labels may well be somewhat different from one country to another.

Regulatory agencies have been increasing the depth and breadth of the information they require, raising their safety standards, intensifying inspections of drug manufacturing processes, and narrowing the indication labels they are willing to approve. This behavior is in direct response to increasing public concerns about drug side effects, the unknown or unmeasurable risks inherent in drugs targeting hitherto unexploited biological pathways and drug targets, and the complex manufacturing processes necessitated by many of the new biologic drugs. Thus, these new drugs must not only meet the higher performance standards demanded by healthcare payers; they must also stand up to a more intense level of regulatory scrutiny.

Management Reductionism and Molecular Reductionism

Biopharma R&D has also been subjected to internal pressures originating in management practices and approaches that focused on project progression over discovery and attempted to routinize R&D at the cost of creativity. In 2008, in the *Harvard Business Review*, Jean-Pierre Garnier, CEO of big pharma GlaxoSmithKline at the time, described some of these problems, asserting that growth in organizational scale and complexity had demotivated and disenfranchised R&D scientists in big pharma.[8] Increased bureaucracy and proactive process management had taken away the incentives for scientific courage and risk taking; the focus of attention had shifted from scientific truth seeking to project progression. The goal was no longer discovery, but moving projects forward to the next review stage. Furthermore, Garnier argued, the leaders of major pharmaceutical corporations had made a gross error in thinking that R&D could be managed as an industrialized, scalable, repeatable process, its management reduced to a focus on detailed process metrics. This mentality, he asserted, had led to a drive for ever-increasing economies of scale and triggered a wave of industry consolidation, the net result of which was, in Garnier's words "a loss of personal accountability, transparency, and the passion of scientists in discovery and development."[9]

These changes are a result of the immense investor pressures faced by large, publicly traded companies. Such companies are expected to deliver predictable profit streams in return for specific expenses, and their cash flows are scrutinized and modeled extensively by independent investment analysts. This scrutiny often leads to top management (consciously or otherwise) regarding individual projects and the overall R&D organization as machines that can be engineered to convert specified inputs into predictable outputs, with productivity enhanced through the control of a small number of key management levers. This thinking, which I refer to as **management reductionism**, is driven by the belief that once the machine has been correctly engineered, its outputs can be increased through corresponding increases in the relevant inputs—in other words, to get more out, you simply throw more money in! Bernard Munos, an executive at big pharma Eli Lilly, noted this trend in another often-quoted paper from 2009:

> During the past couple of decades, there has been a methodical attempt to codify every facet of the drug business into sophisticated processes, in an effort to reduce the variances and increase the predictability. This has produced a false sense of control over all aspects of the pharmaceutical enterprise, including innovation.[10]

The management reductionism mindset was further reinforced in the 1990s by the scientific popularity of the philosophy of **molecular reductionism**, which argues that disease is best treated by first identifying and then appropriately modulating the action of a single molecule, the drug target, along a specific human **biological pathway**.[11] The widespread adoption of the philosophy of molecular reductionism led many life scientists to believe that there was one best way to treat a particular disease, and that was to adopt the following systematic three-step approach:

1) Identify the single biological pathway that is most relevant to the disease in question;
2) Determine the best **mechanism of action** for influencing that pathway by modulating a specific biological molecule (the drug target) that acts along that pathway in a way that is relevant to the disease; and
3) Create a patentable new molecule (candidate drug) that biochemically binds to the drug target to alter its function, thus changing the behavior of the biological pathway and altering the progress of the disease.

The combination of management reductionism and molecular reductionism was temptingly attractive to the leaders of the big pharmas, as well as their management consultants and bankers. Beginning in the 1990s, the big pharmas invested huge sums in building industrialized R&D machines that aimed, using a brute force approach, to systematically identify molecular drug targets and then generate new drug compounds via a scalable industrial process. However, the underlying complexities of biological pathways and drug targets spawned highly unpredictable and challenging R&D projects that were not amenable to such an approach. To make matters worse, industrialization of R&D also served to negatively affected creativity, innovation, and decision making by R&D scientists and their managers.

The result was a critical loss in productivity. As Munos demonstrates, the number of NMEs approved by the FDA by all companies essentially followed a statistical Poisson distribution from 1950 to 2008,[12] reflecting the drug discovery and early-stage R&D model prevalent between approximately 1940 and 2000—that is, the traditional, fully integrated, in-house model. In other words, the generation of new drugs over time by a company occurred at a constant (although stochastically variable) rate regardless of the size of the company. This explains why, as the industry consolidated into a smaller number of very large companies, the total number of approved NMEs discovered by the large companies fell.

Most of the growth in value during this period came from **blockbuster drugs**—highly effective treatments for widespread medical needs that yielded high volumes at high prices, at least for as long as their patents lasted. But blockbuster drugs are essentially random occurrences; the probability of any individual company discovering one is very low. They cannot be programmed in advance, despite the best efforts of blockbuster inventors to rationalize their success with the benefit of hindsight. They are, in other words, classic black swans.[13]

Thus, the implementation of seemingly straightforward approaches—to both scientific and management challenges—turned out to be much harder than anticipated. Scientifically, molecular reductionism proved to be a limited approach for a whole range of reasons. Many potential drug targets have **druggability** challenges, meaning that they may not be amenable to having drug molecules bind to them. Even when a drug molecule can be made to bind to a target, the physical and chemical characteristics of the drug needed sometimes made the resulting candidate drug impractical, in terms of drug absorption and excretion rates or distribution and metabolism mechanisms needed for acceptably safe dosage levels.

Candidate drugs also sometimes produced **off-target effects**—specific kinds of side effects caused by a candidate drug binding to other molecules besides the one it was designed for. Off-target binding can play havoc with all manner of other biological pathways and cause unintended side effects. Alternatively, the drug target itself may play an unexpected role in an altogether different function in the body, again leading to unexpected side effects. In some cases, successful deactivation of one biological pathway by a candidate drug triggered the activation of previously dormant **backup pathways**, thus negating the effect of the candidate drug.

And finally, some diseases are simply very challenging, with etiologies that are complex and poorly understood. For example, in the 413 clinical trials for Alzheimer's disease conducted worldwide from 2002 to 2012, there was a 99.6% failure rate.[14]

The diversity and magnitude of these scientific challenges meant that projects were simply not amenable to industrialized, process-oriented R&D management approaches. Strict gated development approaches didn't allow for the detours and iterations that science sometimes requires. New ways of thinking about R&D and creating value were clearly needed.

The Light at the End of the Tunnel

One of those new approaches—**precision medicine**—has emerged from another common problem in the molecular reductionism philosophy. Sometimes, researchers found that what had been regarded as a single disease turned out to be a group of disease variants that exhibited similar outward symptoms but had different underlying causes at the molecular level. For example, leukemia comprises a group of diseases with over a dozen variants, all of which exhibit the same symptoms of cancer in the blood cells but whose individual etiologies involve varying sets of pathways and interactions. So when a candidate drug modulating a specific drug target along a specific pathway was tested on the whole disease population (as traditionally defined), the aggregate results were often statistically inconclusive since only the subpopulation with the relevant variant was affected. In this context, conducting sensible clinical research requires identifying accurate biomarkers and practical diagnostic tests to identify patients with a particular disease variant; this is known as **patient stratification**.

Precision medicine, or **personalized medicine**, relies on precise patient stratification to target drugs not just to a disease but to a particular variant of a disease. Although precision medicine increases R&D complexity while reducing the size of the relevant patient subpopulation, creating additional marketing challenges, it offers significant opportunities as well. The more targeted approach should reduce the cost of clinical trial programs, and, as scientists get better at targeting relevant subpopulations and trials, should produce more precise results—and the kind of performance payers increasingly demand. Precision medicine is increasingly being adopted as a way to demonstrate high impact in a tightly defined patient subpopulation, and thus to justify a price that allows the company to recoup its R&D investment and justify the risks of continued R&D. As a result, the approach has been enthusiastically embraced by biopharma companies and healthcare payers alike over the past few years.

The emergence of the partnering model for R&D is another promising sign. As Munos argues, diversity of ideas and approaches drives innovation, even highly unpredictable blockbuster innovation. The best way to ensure future blockbusters is to simply have more shots on goal, more thoughtful projects driven by as diverse a range of researchers as possible. Small companies and academic research institutes provide a large part of that required diversity, and are thus engines for innovation:

> By virtue of their number, small firms collectively can explore far more directions, and investigate areas that their larger, more conservative competitors avoid. However, only a small fraction of these small companies will be rewarded with an FDA approval. So individually, [smaller firms are] a much less reliable source of NMEs than large companies, but collectively, they produce more, for less.[15]

The new paradigm of collaborative innovation is a reflection of the industry's realization of the importance of diversity in innovation. Companies pursuing externalization, outsourcing, and partnerships across their R&D value chains are essentially pursuing a strategy of diversity through **networked R&D**.

That strategy is beginning to pay off. The partnering trend really began to accelerate ten to fifteen years ago, and the first light is appearing at the end of the tunnel: in 2014, 53 new drugs were approved by the FDA, an all-time high beating the previous record of 51, set in 1996. Furthermore, analysis by various industry observers indicates that the value of these approved drugs is also rising strongly.[16]

The pursuit of R&D diversity has an upside for SMEs and academic researchers, too. As more companies realize the benefits of this networked R&D approach, opportunities for smaller organizations to engage in asymmetric partnerships with big pharmas—and access big pharma resources to bring their ideas to market—will only grow.

Chapter Notes

[1] See Tufts Center for Drug Development, "Cost to Develop and Win Marketing Approval for a New Drug Is $2.6 Billion," press release, November 18, 2014, http://csdd.tufts.edu/news/complete_story/pr_tufts_csdd_2014_cost_study.

[2] D. Cook, D. Brown, R. Alexander, R. March, P. Morgan, G. Satterthwaite, and M. N. Pangalos, "Lessons Learned from the Fate of AstraZeneca's Drug Pipeline," *Nature Reviews Drug Discovery* 13 (2014): 419–431, http://www.nature.com/nrd/journal/v13/n6/full/nrd4309.html.

[3] J. W. Scannell, A. Blanckley, H. Boldon, and B. Warrington, "Diagnosing the Decline in Pharmaceutical R&D Efficiency," *Nature Reviews Drug Discovery* 11 (March 2012): 191–200. See especially the charts at http://www.nature.com/nrd/journal/v11/n3/fig_tab/nrd3681_F1.html.

[4] F. Pammolli, L. Magazzini, and M. Riccaboni, "The Productivity Crisis in Pharmaceutical R&D," *Nature Reviews Drug Discovery* 10 (June 2011): 428–438.

[5] Pammolli et al., "The Productivity Crisis" (2011), p. 438.

[6] Scannell et al., "Diagnosing the Decline" (2012), p. 193.

[7] Scannell et al., "Diagnosing the Decline" (2012), p. 194.

[8] Jean-Pierre Garnier, "Rebuilding the R&D Engine in Big Pharma," *Harvard Business Review* 86, no. 5 (May 2008): 68–76.

[9] Garnier, "Rebuilding the R&D Engine" (2008), p. 76.

[10] Bernard Munos, "Lessons from 60 Years of Pharmaceutical Innovation," *Nature Reviews Drug Discovery* 8 (December 2009): 959–968. Quotation, p. 967.

[11] For one description of this approach, see M. H. V. Van Regenmortel, "Reductionism and Complexity in Molecular Biology," *EMBO Reports* 5, no. 11 (November 2004): 1016–1020.

[12] Munos, "Lessons from 60 Years" (2009), p. 961.

[13] A black swan is an event that comes as a surprise, has a major effect, and is often inappropriately rationalized after the fact. See N. N. Taleb, *The Black Swan: The Impact of the Highly Improbable* (New York: Random House, 2007).

[14] J. Cummings, T. Morstorf, and K. Zhong, "Alzheimer's Disease Drug-Development Pipeline: Few Candidates, Frequent Failures," *Alzheimer's Research & Therapy* 6, no. 4, p. 37, http://www.alzres.com/content/6/4/37.

[15] Munos, "Lessons from 60 Years" (2009), p. 965.

[16] See, for example, Ulrik Schulze, Mathias Bädeker, Yen Ting Chen, and David Greber, "R&D Productivity 2014: A Breakthrough Year for Biopharma," *BCG Perspectives*, February 13, 2015, https://www.bcgperspectives.com/content/articles/biopharmaceuticals_innovation_r_and_d_productivity_2014_breakthrough_year/.

Chapter 3
The Benefits and Risks of Partnering

The distinctive characteristics of biopharma R&D—risky, expensive projects shaped by scientific complexity and economic and regulatory pressures—have negatively affected R&D productivity in the industry. Recent developments suggest that a partnering approach can help reverse that trend, by providing big pharma companies access to new ideas and expertise and giving smaller organizations access to the market. However, the full benefits of partnering do not come without costs, in the form of heightened risk and added investment of both time and money. These additional benefits and risks need to shared as part of the partnership agreement.

In this chapter, we will look at both the benefits and the additional risks of working collaboratively. In particular, we introduce the important notions of execution risk, collaboration risk, and the collaboration tax. We close the chapter by describing the typical financial mechanisms used in formal partnership agreements to share risks and returns.

The Benefits of Partnering

Partnering clearly is a boon to the biopharma industry, and to healthcare as a whole. Partnering can provide important benefits to the participating organizations as well; Goliath and David each turn to partnering for different reasons, seeking different benefits and driven by different needs. For both Goliath and David, the interaction of their distinctive capabilities and experience bases should create synergy, leading to broad organizational outcomes beyond the results of the immediate project, including:

- Better ideas and more creative thinking, leading to superior innovations.
- Improved problem solving in terms of both speed and solution quality.
- Stimulation of in-house operational improvements via observing how others do things.

For Goliath, the primary driver for partnering is the corporation's embrace of a networked R&D strategy based on diversity. The Goliath company recognizes that sharing a project with an external partner will bring in ideas, expertise, technologies, and management capabilities that supplement its internal efforts and improve its overall R&D outcomes. To increase diversity and spread risk, it will usually manage a portfolio of many such R&D alliances with a variety of different partners.

Goliath's engagement with partners and potential partners will be driven by its internal focus strategies—its decision to concentrate its efforts in certain therapeutic, product, or other areas. It will only make alliances that fit this focus and maximize its chances of success in those targeted areas. It will also have decided to focus its internal R&D operations on efforts tightly connected to those targets and will therefore maintain a portfolio of service and technology provider partnerships as well. These provider partnerships both bring in specialist expertise and technologies to support internal projects and ensure a flexible, scalable resource base. Even though most Goliaths continue to retain in-house project portfolios and maintain a baseline of in-house operational resources, most also regularly choose to partner on individual projects or outsource individual functions, knowing that in aggregate they are aiming for a certain level of externalization.

For David, partnering with a Goliath is usually not optional but compulsory, the only choice being which individual partner and what specific deal to agree to. The primary driver is often the need for funding and resources. Partnering is built into the business model of most Davids; Goliath partners represent not just providers of cash flow but also channels to the marketplace. Another important driver for David is access to specialist capabilities it cannot maintain in-house, for reasons related to scale economy or the business model. A David of sufficient scale will also maintain a portfolio of partnerships to balance risks and provide access to a breadth of different market opportunities.

The Risks of Partnering

While partnering may offer substantial benefits over going it alone, it does not come without risks. Some of these risks are common to R&D projects across industries; others are peculiar to biopharma or to collaborations.

The traditional approach to managing risk in R&D projects is founded on the twin notions of **scientific risk** and **commercial risk**. The reasons usually given when a biopharma R&D project fails fall into these categories. Take for instance these common explanations for a project's abandonment:

- Insufficient efficacy.
- Unacceptable side effects.
- Not competitive with other expected prescriber options.
- Inability to achieve an acceptable level of reimbursement and pricing.

The first two reasons represent scientific risk—the project cannot achieve its technical aims. The last two reflect commercial risk—the technical aims are achievable (for instance, the drug does kills cancer cells with acceptable side effects), but the project cannot be successful commercially; it cannot outperform competitors. Projects normally have both types of risks assessed before they get the go-ahead to proceed. The normal mechanism for mitigating these risks during project execution is to assemble at the outset project resources (team members, governance committee members, advisers, contractors) that have the most appropriate and relevant expertise and experience in both the scientific and the commercial arenas.

Beyond these common risks, biopharma collaborations also face heightened execution risk and a set of collaboration risks that are inherent to the partnership approach.

Execution Risk

In addition to scientific and commercial risks, the peculiarities and project dynamics of biopharma R&D introduce a high degree of what I call **execution risk**—the risk arising from being unable to resolve unanticipated problems or exploit unanticipated opportunities over the course of the project's execution. While execution risk is of course present in R&D projects for all industries, it is particularly high in biopharma, especially in the early and middle stages of a project, which span disease research, drug discovery, preclinical development, and exploratory clinical development. It is in these phases that emerging science, changing regulator requirements, fluctuating payer priorities, evolving medical treatment paradigms, and periodic organizational restructuring lead to a long and windy road to commercialization, characterized by unexpected outcomes, dead ends, and sidetracks. Much of the risk of failure in this context relates to factors unknown, uncontrollable, or not well understood at the outset of the project. This is execution risk, and it is very high in biopharma. Given this high risk, merely assembling project resources with historical experience of the known scientific and commercial issues is not by itself a sufficient strategy for success. There are simply too many variables—some of them not even identifiable at a project's outset—all contributing to the very low observed probabilities of success in biopharma R&D!

Those biopharma projects that do deal effectively with the high execution risk succeed through adaptation and creative problem solving. Project teams respond effectively and efficiently to new problems or opportunities as they emerge by, for example:

- Adapting the project activity plan in real time.
- Bringing in new expertise or resources that are needed, while releasing those that are no longer relevant.
- Innovating new solutions through a process of co-creation and creative conflict among team members.

As a counterpoint, I have observed three factors that intensify execution risk. First, any deficiencies in the communication, problem-solving, or decision-making capabilities of the project team inhibits adaptation. Second, an inflexible project management approach will limit the capacity of the team to respond to new challenges and thus increase execution risk. The conventional project management paradigm of adhering strictly to preset deliverables, timelines, and activity budgets can cause more harm than good in situations with high execution risk. What matters is getting to the goal, rather than how to get there. Sadly, I have seen too many projects stalled or even cancelled because the team was not allowed to adopt a more nimble, adaptive project path.

Third, overly narrow project goals reduce the chances of significant new value emerging from the project. Many projects generate scientific findings that have much broader applicability than the original scope would allow. But if everyone is fixated on a narrowly defined set of goals, these insights, and the opportunities associated with them, can be missed. There are many success stories of canceled drug projects that were rescued through reformulation or repurposing by other companies. And what about the many rejected early-stage compounds that were never tested for other applications? Or the possibility of discovering innovative biomarkers during a research program investigating a new disease mechanism? These outcomes are too often classified as failures, and the new knowledge inherent in these "failures" is lost.

Collaboration Risk

When we conduct biopharma R&D projects in a partnership context, we also see the emergence of what I call **collaboration risk**—the incremental risk arising from the added complications of working with one or more external partners. Collaboration risk manifests itself in two different ways: intensified execution risk, and orphaning of the project by one of the partners.

Collaboration risk is especially high in David & Goliath partnerships in which the asymmetries between the two parties interfere with the adaptation and creative problem solving required to mitigate execution risk.

Elevated execution risk often arises from fundamental differences in organizational missions, processes, and culture that create confusion and tension. Stark differences in decision-making process and speed, as well as cultural norms and values, between David and Goliath (and, in the case of Goliath, even from one part of the organization to another) can hamper decision making and leave project teams unsure how to move forward.

There is also often a huge gap in power and risk perception. Goliath, which provides most if not all of the funding, maintains a large portfolio of both internal and partnered projects that it will prioritize over time, terminating some in the process. But David needs the partnership for cash flow and to build stakeholder credibility. Being terminated, put on hold, or delayed by Goliath's portfolio management process could threaten its very existence—what is for Goliath just "business as usual" is a matter of life or death for David.

Partner needs may differ in other ways, as well. For example, academic researchers must publish their research to further their careers, and most small biotech companies need a stream of news flow to grow enterprise valuation and support investor fund-raising. A large multinational firm, on the other hand, might prefer to keep its proprietary research and early development results under wraps until the resulting products are close to the marketplace.

The structure of the project may also introduce tensions that increase execution risk. Unlike projects housed within a single company, partnerships operate under shared leadership. The joint project team (JPT), joint steering committee (JSC), and other project structures will often be composed of parallel leaders for each of the various functions—one from each organization involved in the partnership. This practice ensures sufficient oversight and clear communication channels to allow each side to understand what the other is doing and learning. However, it can also become a source of frustration if the two individuals assigned to a function are misaligned or at odds with each other.

One source of execution risk is the changes in personnel that occur over the course of a long project. This is a factor in collaborations, as well, particularly in the hand-off from the deal team to the execution team. Many partnerships are the consummation of a mating process that may have taken many months and absorbed the energy and attention of key individuals from both sides. Once the deal is done, however, many of those involved in its negotiation will move on to focus on other deals. The JPT that is charged with executing the collaboration is often left bereft of anyone who was heavily involved in crafting the deal; more often than not, the only continuity is provided by some individuals on the JSC, which is less involved in the day-to-day execution of the project. Important tacit insights may be lost in the transition from deal to execution, and the JPT will often struggle to internalize the spirit of the collaboration, its broader underlying aims and rationale, relying instead on the formal project plan and deliverables to guide their work, a focus that may create myopia and hamper flexibility.

There is also a psychological hand-off as well. In both David and Goliath, immediate personal recognition and organizational bragging rights often come from finding and doing the deal. From a cultural standpoint, the challenge of execution is often undervalued and not given sufficient management attention until something goes badly wrong, by which time it is often too late anyway. This culture can leave JPTs to struggle without the organizational attention the deal-making team received.

All these factors combine to create a high potential for misunderstanding and miscommunication on both technical and procedural aspects of the project, greatly intensifying the execution risk. It is challenging enough to instill a nimble, adaptive project management approach with a team drawn from many different functions in the same company. The bar is an order of magnitude higher when the project team and its governance process include cross-functional participants from two different organizations with very different missions and culture.

Even if the JPT works effectively and efficiently to minimize the execution risk, there is nevertheless a potential for a collaboration to become isolated from one of its parent organizations, typically the Goliath partner. This is especially likely if:

- The topic or nature of the collaboration is unusual or seen to be inconsequential relative to norms of the parent organization or its stated primary goals.
- The individuals participating in the collaboration are neither particularly influential nor well networked in their parent organizations. As the CEO of a David biotech company said to me, "Having worked with this large pharma on several projects, we definitely prefer some of their project leaders and alliance managers rather than others—the best ones are those that network into their own organization to get help and to sell what the project is doing, while the worst ones are those whom their own organization ignores."

If a collaboration becomes orphaned, the most appropriate skills and resources in Goliath may not be brought into play, severely limiting the collaboration's potential. Furthermore, the collaboration has a higher risk of being deprioritized in Goliath's portfolio review process, as key decision makers may not understand its true value. Even if the project is completed successfully, its learnings and outputs may not be fully exploited by Goliath.

In my experience, the root causes of collaboration risk are primarily people and culture related, including lack of mutual understanding, poor interpersonal relationships, a "not invented here" mindset, and self-centered behaviors. I have often heard people blame "poor personal chemistry" or having "picked the wrong partner" for collaborations breaking down. But in many of these cases, the partners just had not put in enough effort to make the partnership work.

The more asymmetric the partnership, the more necessary it is to make a concerted effort to build mutual understanding, else confusion could reign or distrust could grow. Personal relationships at all levels of the collaboration are the most important mechanism to improve mutual understanding and enhance problem-solving capacity. Selecting the right actors to be the front-facing individuals and giving them the necessary support is key to mitigating collaboration risk.

The right actors have several important characteristics. First an open mindset is absolutely necessary in a good collaborator. If the people involved in collaborations are not receptive to others' ideas and ways of doing things, the collaboration risk is increased substantially. Similarly, a tendency to compete with or try to show up one's counterparts from the other side can increase tension, and a tendency to control how the partner does things can be counterproductive, as well.

Ultimately, good collaboration partners must recognize the need for win-win behaviors and an element of give and take. One senior scientist who has been involved in a lot of partnerships summarized this viewpoint to me: "You have to be willing to give up some things in order to get the extra benefits from collaborating. You can't have too much pride in your own expertise or assume that you can always do everything the way you would like to." An experienced alliance manager I spoke with offered a similar view: "The value comes from each partner bringing different pieces to the table. But working together also brings potentially conflicting approaches. So you have to be open to it and manage it."

The Collaboration Tax

Partnering could well be the solution to the biopharma industry's R&D productivity woes. But it does not come for free! The heightened execution risk and additional collaboration risk produce a **collaboration tax** that all partnerships incur, comprising the additional costs and risks that partnerships bring compared to purely in-house efforts.[1] In deciding whether and with whom to partner, both David and Goliath partners must take this tax into consideration, and allow for it when estimating ROI and allocating resources to the project.

But consideration of the collaboration tax happens all too infrequently. Even as partnerships have become more pervasive in biopharma, I still observe organizations entering into external partnerships without clearly understanding or allowing for the full risks and costs of doing so. In partnerships I have had the privilege to be involved in, I have seen Goliath organizations expend significant resources in due diligence, often engaging an army of internal and external experts to assess the scientific and commercial risks of the proposed endeavor. Much senior management attention on both sides is devoted to discussing the due diligence results and negotiating the deal terms accordingly. But once execution commences, attention and investment wane. Resources fade away, and little management attention is devoted to the added execution and collaboration risks—until the first major item of bad news emerges from the collaboration. This is the result of a failure to recognize and account for the collaboration tax.

Many of the larger biopharma companies, recognizing the additional burden at least to some extent, have assigned alliance managers to support partnerships. This is an important step to minimize the impact of the collaboration tax. However, although alliance managers have a critical role to play in facilitating action and supporting project teams, many of the actions required to mitigate these risks require active participation by members of the project team or governance committee. Thus, interpersonal relationships within and across partner organizations remain critical.

However, even stellar project teams with strong relationships and wide networks cannot completely eliminate the collaboration tax. Rather, in designing partnerships, organizations must ensure that the projects have the potential to generate a substantially higher return than in-house projects with equivalent scientific and commercial risks. This applies to both joint product innovation partnerships and valued-added outsourcing partnerships.

This line of thinking leads to two key implications for those embarking on partnerships:

- The ROI hurdle for the potential return from a collaboration should be higher than that for an in-house project, all other factors being equal.
- The return from a collaboration should be enhanced by (a) transferring relevant experience and know-how generated by the partnership to other projects or parts of the organization, and (b) allowing flexibility to alter the collaboration's goals if the original premise becomes no longer viable.

Considering these factors at the outset will allow for a better decision-making process up front. At the same time, those entering into an asymmetric partnership, from either the David or the Goliath side, would do well to act early on to mitigate risk and minimize the collaboration tax, by selecting JPT and JSC members carefully and providing the project team with ample support and flexibility. Finally, partnership arrangements should be designed to incorporate more resources for mitigating the collaboration tax.

Sharing Risks and Returns

Sharing the anticipated higher returns net of all the costs—including the collaboration tax—is an important aspect of the partnership agreement. The typical endgame of many R&D collaborations is that Goliath will ultimately drive the global commercialization of any resulting innovations and products, the roots of which are provided by David. So most of the financial mechanisms for sharing returns represent a transfer of financial value from Goliath to David.

We focus here on the nomenclature and key characteristics of these mechanisms; a more detailed assessment of their merits, weaknesses, and nuances is beyond the scope of this book.[2]

Many partnerships start with an up-front payment, or **signing fee**, from Goliath to David, payable on signature of the partnership agreement. This payment usually reflects the investment David has already made in the idea or technology the collaboration will develop, whether protected through patents or otherwise. The signing fee may be used as an incentive in a competitive situation in which David has multiple Goliath suitors.

In addition, Goliath often agrees to provide most or all of the needed **R&D operational funding** (funds needed to cover what are variously called *research costs, development costs*, or *FTE costs*) incurred by the project as the collaboration progresses. These payments may or may not include a transparent margin over David's actual out-of-pocket expenditure. Where David is an academic laboratory or nonprofit research institute, this kind of payment is commonly referred to as a grant.

Further payments from Goliath to David may be contingent on the collaboration achieving specific outcomes or reaching particular development goals; these are **milestone payments**. Goliath may also agree to make additional **performance bonus payments** if the milestone is achieved at a higher quality or performance level than a defined minimum.

If intellectual property (IP) has been licensed from one party to another, the licensee may pay **royalties** to the licensor for the use of that IP. Royalties can be payable during development, especially if the IP is in the form of research-enabling technology, or when the resulting product is marketed, especially if the IP is in the form of a patented molecule or delivery technology used in the product. In the latter case, the royalties due are typically expressed as a percentage of the net revenue—that is, product revenue after deducting distributor and customer discounts.

Once the product generated by the collaboration reaches the market, David may also receive **revenue share** or **profit share** payments. A revenue share has the same effect as a royalty on revenue but is not tied to any specific IP; a profit share is a fixed proportion of what is left from revenue after production, distribution, marketing, and sales costs have been deducted. Royalties, revenue shares, and profit shares are all expressed as a percentage of net revenues or net profits. Those percentages may be fixed or they may be tiered, paid on a sliding scale depending on various conditions or the satisfaction of specific performance requirements.

If David has been a key driver in developing the manufacturing process as well as the product itself, it may capture additional financial value after product launch by manufacturing the product. In this scenario, Goliath buys the active ingredient or finished dosage forms from David, with the pricing for this **cost of goods (COGS) arrangement** usually incorporating a profit margin for David.

For Goliath, one goal is to ensure it receives value in return for its payments to David. One increasingly popular mechanism to achieve this is for Goliath to receive **equity** (or equity-like instruments such as options or similar financial derivatives) in David as part of the deal. The exchange of equity can be structured so that an up-front or milestone payment represents a purchase of shares (or options). For Goliath, this is a bet on the success of the project; if the resulting product is successful (or even with positive news at later-stage milestones), the value of this investment will often shoot up dramatically.

The ultimate financial mechanism for consolidating value from the collaboration is of course an outright acquisition of David by Goliath. This can and does happen when Goliath desires outright control over the fruits of the collaboration, either because it wants to protect its interests in a highly competitive market or because it feels the acquisition price is cheaper than the financial net present value (NPV) of the future payments it expects to make to David.

A final source of financial value is the **marketing rights** to the product. Marketing rights are a more indirect mechanism for sharing value, as they represent only the right to sell the product rather than a direct transfer of funds. In some cases, David may negotiate the right to sell the product resulting from a collaboration in certain geographical territories, whether as the exclusive seller in that area or as Goliath's marketing partner.

Many of the financial mechanisms used in partnership agreements are contingent on progress. These payments, which David will receive only if certain things happen, are often referred to as **bio-dollars**. Some of the contingencies for which bio-dollars may be offered, especially additional registered indications and higher tiered sales milestones, may never occur even if the collaboration results in a successful product launch. Both the David negotiator and the uninformed press release reader need to be wary of the bio-dollar hype!

In practice, most partnership agreements will include only some of these mechanisms, and what we've covered here represents only the baseline. Many agreements implement variants of these arrangements to accommodate the specific circumstances of the partnership, the innovation, and the parties involved. Ultimately, the financial arrangements must not only fit the needs of the individual partners but also acknowledge the specific risks, rewards, and challenges of that particular collaboration.

Chapter Notes

[1] What I call a collaboration tax is sometimes referred to by other industry analysts and consultants as a *partnering tax* or an *alliance tax*.

[2] See for example B. Bogdan and R. Villiger, *Valuation in Life Sciences: A Practical Guide*, 3rd edition (Heidelberg, Germany: Springer-Verlag Berlin, 2010).

CHAPTER 4
BILATERAL R&D PARTNERSHIP MODELS

Although the financial arrangements are important in ensuring David captures fair value from its innovations, there are a plethora of issues to consider in designing a David & Goliath partnership.[1] How the two parties work with each other will depend on the scientific domain of inquiry, the market context, and both partners' capabilities and aims. Because it defines the relationship between the two parties, the design of the partnership is critically important to the ultimate success of the collaboration.

In this chapter, we look at the different models for bilateral R&D partnerships in the biopharma sector to illustrate the diversity of approaches that have been implemented and provide a useful shorthand for use in later discussion. First, we introduce a framework for classifying partnership designs that I have found particularly helpful in setting up and managing David & Goliath partnerships. We explore practical examples of each model, highlight their distinctive features and outline the prerequisites for success in each one. At the end of the chapter, we highlight some key dos and don'ts for designing partnerships.

Classifying Bilateral R&D Partnerships

There are four different mechanisms by which value is created and transferred in a bilateral, David & Goliath R&D partnership:

- *Value-added supply.* David supplies a product or service to one or more of Goliath's R&D projects in a way that adds unique value that would not be created with a typical **commodity supplier**.
- *IP transfer.* David transfers previously developed IP to Goliath, which then uses that IP in one or more of its R&D projects.
- *Sponsored R&D program.* Goliath funds one or more R&D projects conducted by David; the projects are operated by David's people and David's subcontractors and suppliers.
- *Joint endeavor.* Both David and Goliath people are significantly involved in day-to-day R&D operations and decision making and contribute jointly to value creation and project development.

Each of these mechanisms has two or three variants, which are primarily distinguishable by the amount of interaction between the participants (Figure 4.1). Each model, and each variant, has its own approach to operations and decision making. In the discussion that follows, financial mechanisms are mentioned only when they are distinguishing features of the model; there will usually be other financial mechanisms that are not explicitly mentioned.

Figure 4.1. **Bilateral R&D Partnership Models and Variants**

Model	Low ← Extent & Frequency of Interaction → Very High			
Value-Added Supply	Preferred Provider	Customized Supply	Collaborative Supply	
IP Transfer	Over the Wall	Originator Involvement		
Sponsored R&D Program	Hands Off	Operational Sponsor		
Joint Endeavor		Pass the Baton	Divide and Conquer	Co-Creative

Value-Added Supply

In many biopharma R&D organizations, the outsourcing of certain non-core R&D operations (such as, for instance, chemical reference compound synthesis, *in vivo* preclinical toxicology testing, and clinical data monitoring) is now an accepted fact of life. Some of this outsourcing relates to standardized activities that could be delivered by any of a range of different external suppliers; these contracts are regarded by the parties involved as straight buyer-seller transactions. But there is also a significant number of supplier arrangements that are truly partnerships in the sense that both sides see themselves as engaged in a collaborative long-term win-win relationship with the other. These value-added supply arrangements come in three variants: preferred provider partnerships, customized supply arrangements, and collaborative supply arrangements.

Preferred Provider Partnerships

Preferred provider partnerships (sometimes called *preferred supplier partnerships*) are arrangements in which a CRO and its biopharma customer closely integrate operations, creating cost and time savings for the customer. The preferred CRO, which is regarded by the customer as a collaborator, is offered better terms than competitors because *how* the services are delivered adds value beyond the type of services supplied. Several pharma R&D managers expressed the benefits of such arrangements in similar terms; as one told me, "There are CROs offering the same services, some even at lower unit prices, but we prefer to work with our preferred suppliers as the total cost incurred is lower, things happen quicker, and the quality of information transfer is better."

Example—Preferred Provider Partnership

CRO D1 conducts standard *in vivo* preclinical toxicology studies required in the regulatory application for a candidate drug's first human trials. Over time, it has developed a long-standing relationship with multinational pharma company G1 and a deep understanding of G1's specific priorities and needs in interpreting data from *in vivo* experiments. D1 trains its people to work with G1's processes and culture, has integrated its laboratory information systems with those of G1 to achieve seamless data transfer, and has adopted Good Laboratory Practice (GLP) standards that align closely with the preferences of G1's quality assurance group.

So, although a multitude of other providers offer the same studies as D1, D1 has a preferred supplier partnership arrangement with G1 that includes a pricing scheme with volume discounts; committed minimum volumes; mutual investments to integrate processes and systems; and problem-solving forums, training, and information-sharing activities. In essence, D1 operates as a seamless extension of G1's internal processes while providing the benefits of an external provider, such as scale economies and specialist knowledge.

Customized Supply Arrangements

Some pharma customers would prefer to outsource key, noncore functions but require that services be significantly customized for their individual circumstances and requirements. For these customers, CROs may engage in **customized supply arrangements** under which a high degree of value-adding customer specificity is incorporated into the services provided. The design process for these services involves significant customer-supplier interaction—the customer briefs the supplier on its needs and collaborates with it to finalize the service design. Confusingly, these arrangements are also sometimes referred to as preferred provider arrangements, reflecting the preferential deal struck between the parties.

Example—Customized Supply Arrangement

D2 is an academic research laboratory with unique access to arthritic joint tissue samples. The lab has deep expertise in developing biological assays of those tissue samples. Multinational pharma G2 needs a customized *ex vivo* assay that focuses on a particular biological pathway and, subsequently, wants to test a series of potential drug candidates in this assay. G2 contracts with D2 to provide the specific assay and tests it requires, collaborating with the lab to develop the tests and providing a favorable reimbursement and other benefits in return.

Collaborative Supply Arrangements

In yet another variant of value-added supply, even the delivery process is collaborative. In **collaborative supply arrangements**, the customer participates not only in the design but also in the delivery of the customized services. Under these arrangements, customer and CRO personnel work closely together to design and execute tests or other services, ensuring the customer's specific needs are met. The CRO adds value in the form of unique expertise or equipment.

Example—Collaborative Supply Arrangement

D3 is a chemistry CRO contracted to synthesize a succession of drug-like compounds over the duration of a discovery project being conducted by multinational pharma G3. At regular intervals, G3's medicinal chemists consult with their D3 counterparts to design the next batch of molecules that D3 will synthesize. The synthesized compounds are then shipped to G3's laboratory for testing in various assays developed by G3's biologists; the assay results are subsequently used to inform the next round of collaborative molecule design.

Building a Successful Value-Added Supply Arrangement

Value-added supply arrangements are relatively straightforward. In all such arrangements, there is a clear seller and a clear buyer; ownership of whatever is produced by the supplier passes to the customer when the relevant fees are paid. There are no questions around IP or other complex value-transfer mechanisms.

However, there are some prerequisites both customer and supplier should consider to ensure a successful relationship:

- The customer must be clear about what it wants to achieve, without trying to dictate how it thinks the results should be delivered. A good value-added supplier often has more experience in relevant areas and better ideas for how best to deliver a defined outcome.
- The supplier must allocate time and resources to fully understand what the customer wants to achieve, rather than simply taking a list of desired service or product parameters at face value.

- The customer must allocate time and resources to help the supplier customize and deliver the contracted services, even when the supplier does most of the work.
- The customer needs to recognize that the best supplier for its needs is not just one with the relevant technical skills but also one with whom it can collaborate closely. The customer should be open to paying a premium in return for a higher-value outcome.
- The supplier must have a reasonable chance of actually delivering what the customer wants—too often, wishful thinking on either or both sides combined with a lack of clarity about what is needed lead to failure.

Value-added supply arrangements are one way that pharma companies diversify and network their R&D operations and focus internal resources on key areas of expertise. Both the pharma customers and the CROs can benefit by being flexible in their approach and willing to engage closely with each other to understand the pharma company's specific needs and the CRO's true range of capabilities.

IP Transfer

Small biotech firms, technology providers, and academic research groups working on innovative approaches frequently develop IP of their own, and associated know-how. This IP can become the seed of a drug discovery or development project, or it can solve a technical problem in an existing pharma company's project. In these cases, one common partnering mechanism is for the IP owner to transfer the IP to the pharma company via a licensing agreement, allowing the pharma company to deploy the IP in its R&D projects. **IP transfer** can take place under two different scenarios, reflecting different levels of post-transfer interaction between the two partners: over-the-wall and originator involvement.

Over the Wall

In the **over-the-wall** variant of the IP transfer model, interaction is minimal. There might be some intense exchanges at the outset of the agreement, when the originator (licensor) transfers its know-how, but the recipient (licensee) then uses the IP with little or no involvement on the part of the originator.

Example—Over-the-Wall IP Transfer

D4 is a drug discovery technology provider that has developed a proprietary library of antibodies with specific properties. It has licensed this library to pharma company G4 for use in G4's drug discovery projects, in return for a signing fee and a schedule of royalty payments. After an initial technology transfer and training effort from D4, G4 will continue on its own to utilize D4's library within the terms of the technology licensing agreement.

Originator Involvement

In the **originator involvement** variant of the IP transfer model, there is a much higher degree of ongoing interaction between the originator and the recipient. In these cases, the IP originator continues to stay involved as the recipient implements the IP, owing to some combination of circumstances. Typically, the originator will have specific goals for its involvement, such as:

- Actively monitor and control use of the IP to ensure it is not applied outside the terms of the licensing agreement.
- Provide support and guidance to ensure that maximum value is generated from the IP; this is especially important if the licensing terms include some form of contingent benefit sharing such as royalty payments on future sales.

- Learn about the usability and impact of the IP when it is applied in different situations in order to inspire future improvements.

The level and nature of the originator's involvement will depend on the specific reasons for its remaining involved and the goals of the project.

Example—IP Transfer with Originator Involvement

D5 is a technology provider that has developed a patented technology for injectable delivery of protein drugs based on a revolutionary new approach. Pharma company G5 wishes to license this technology for use with a new class of antibodies it is developing for treating asthma. With this goal in mind, G5 is negotiating with D5 to secure a two-year exclusivity period for its use of the technology; for the initial two years of the arrangement, none of G5's competitors are allowed to work with D5's technology in inflammation-related disease areas. In return, in addition to an up-front signing fee and royalty payments, D5 wants G5 to fund a dedicated team of D5 scientists to work closely with their G5 counterparts over the exclusivity period, with the goals of 1) ensuring that the technology is employed to its best advantage and 2) capturing valuable learnings for future applications and enhancements of the technology.

Building a Successful IP Transfer Arrangement

In the David & Goliath context, the defining characteristics of IP transfer partnerships are:

- David (the originator and licensor of the IP) makes the up-front investment to generate the IP, usually well in advance of knowing to whom precisely it will be transferred.
- The projects in which the IP is applied belong to Goliath (the licensee) and David usually has little or no say in how

those projects are conducted, save for the terms governing how the IP is applied.

An IP transfer deal can be exclusive (only one licensee) or nonexclusive, for a defined duration or in perpetuity, and it may or may not require significant involvement by the licensor in the application of the IP.

With regard to the prerequisites to success, similar comments apply as for the value-added supply models—those contemplating such a deal must be sure to know what they are buying and why. Furthermore, it is important for the licensee to recognize how much originator involvement is needed to ensure the IP is applied most effectively and factor in that cost when evaluating the deal.

Sponsored R&D Program

The **sponsored R&D program**, in which a large pharma company funds a self-contained program of R&D work that is conducted mostly or entirely by a smaller company or academic research group, is another common partnering mechanism. There are, again, two variants to this approach differing primarily in the large company's level of involvement in the research program.

Hands Off

In the **hands-off** program, there is essentially no participation by the sponsoring company in the day-to-day work or operational decision making associated with the research. The sponsor's involvement is limited to a governance role—goal setting, periodic progress reviews, and decision making at key milestones requiring investment of the next major tranche of funds.

Example—Hands-Off Sponsored Program

D6 is a laboratory at a world-renowned university conducting research into multiple sclerosis. After a successful annual review, it is now entering the second year of a three-year grant from pharma company G6 to investigate a defined set of potential drug targets and determine their possible roles in disease etiology and progression. The program is supervised by the laboratory's director, a tenured professor who is the principal investigator for the grant, and the work is carried out by a nominated postdoc supported by two PhD students.

Operational Sponsor

In the **operational sponsor** research program, there is a greater degree of day-to-day participation by the sponsor, which may include contributions in kind (assay transfer, access to compound screening library, or other tools) or even involvement in operational-level decision making.

Example—Sponsored Program with Operational Sponsor

D7 is a drug discovery and preclinical CRO with a full range of biology, chemistry, and pharmacology capabilities. In one of its major customer engagements, it is being sponsored by pharma company G7 to produce a set of candidate drugs for a confidential drug target of G7's choice. G7, which will own all the IP resulting from the project, conducted the initial target validation work and developed unique assays that it has transferred to D7's location. G7 funds the manpower and reagent costs incurred by D7 plus a small margin that is significantly lower than D7's usual pricing level. However, subject to the achievement of specific results on certain timelines, G7 will also pay milestone payments and other performance bonuses; the first two such payments have already been earned and paid. This arrangement represents a risk-sharing mechanism: if the project is successfully completed, the milestone and performance payments will net D7 a much higher total margin than it would have achieved with its usual fee-for-service pricing. While D7 personnel conduct all the work, a G7 team has access to the data being generated and confers with D7's project team every month to make operational decisions jointly as the project progresses.

Building a Successful Sponsored R&D Program

All sponsored R&D programs have one characteristic in common: one party provides all the funding and the other party does most if not all of the work. The sponsor has the final say over how its money is spent and often owns all the data unless (as in many academic collaborations) some of the findings are deemed public domain and published. Each type has its own challenges. In hands-off programs, the sponsor must monitor results closely enough to recognize when pertinent inputs from its people might steer the partner toward outcomes that better suit the sponsor's needs. Conversely, in the operational sponsor variant, sponsors need to focus on how they can add value by complementing the partner's capabilities, rather than trying to control too much in the areas where the partner is strong.

Joint Endeavor

Last but not least are **joint endeavors**, in which, by definition, both parties contribute to the operational effort and collaborate to make key decisions. There are three distinct variants to this approach.

Pass the Baton

In the **pass-the-baton** joint endeavor, one party conducts all the work up to a certain stage of the project while the other party is kept informed on progress. Once the first party's work is complete, operational control passes to the other party, which conducts all the work in subsequent stages while keeping the first party informed. Such an arrangement may work when one partner has strengths in a particular phase of the development process and the other partner has complementary strengths in later phases.

Example—Pass-the-Baton Joint Endeavor

Pharma company G8 has just made the initial signing payment on an agreement with biotech firm D8 to co-develop a candidate drug for colon cancer. The compound has been developed to the preclinical testing stage by D8 and is projected to start its first Phase I/II clinical trials within the next twelve months.

Under the agreement, D8 will continue running the project while keeping G8 updated on progress through the first two planned clinical trials. If those trials are completed with satisfactory outcomes, D8 will earn a large milestone payment from G8, and G8 will then take over the project. G8's work will focus on commercializing the drug, including potentially extending its indications to other solid tumors. If and when the compound reaches the market, D8 will receive royalties on the net sales.

Divide and Conquer

In the **divide-and-conquer** joint endeavor, both parties work concurrently, each with specifically demarcated responsibilities for resources and operational work, sharing data and insights at established milestones. Major decisions about the next set of activities are then made jointly.

Example—Divide-and-Conquer Joint Endeavor

Biotech company D9 and pharma company G9 have agreed to co-develop a topical compound for psoriasis that is about to commence preclinical testing. D9, which discovered the compound in question, has strong expertise in inflammation pathways but lacks dermatology experience; G9 has a long history in dermatology, including several successfully marketed products. G9 has made an initial signing payment to D9 and the two companies have agreed on a development plan in which different parts of the project are allocated to each party; clinical study design and execution is assigned to G9 while active ingredient production and manufacturing process scale-up are assigned to D9. Each party will bear its own costs for the activities it is responsible for. The agreement, which extends through the completion of clinical Phase II trials, establishes a timetable with periodic milestones at which both sides will report back and agree on next actions.

After the compound completes Phase II trials, G9 will own the compound and will take on subsequent costs to launch, and D9 will receive a royalty on future net sales and have a guaranteed contract to manufacture the active ingredient according to an agreed pricing scheme for ten years.

Co-Creative

Finally, the **co-creative** joint endeavor is characterized by a deliberate effort to define, plan, and interpret the key experiments of the project jointly, although at the end of day one side or the other (or even a third-party CRO) physically carries out the experimental work. The aim is to have the partners stimulate and challenge each other in such a way that the resulting solution is more than the sum of the parts.

The co-creative variant requires a much higher frequency of interaction and much greater transparency of details than other models, leading to a greater investment in communication that is hopefully repaid by superior results. In many cases, the distinction between the divide-and-conquer and co-creative variants is a matter of how the project is conducted and the collaborative behavior of its participants—it is quite possible to word the partnership agreement in such a way that either variant could be operated. Hence, this distinction need not be made until operating arrangements are set up by the JSC and the JPT.

Example—Co-Creative Joint Endeavor

D10 is a nonprofit research institute collaborating with large biotech firm G10 to investigate potential drug targets for the treatment of stroke. With the goal of validating at least one innovative drug target within the three-year timeframe of the agreement, the two parties have established a joint team on which participants from both sides work together at an operational level, communicating on a daily basis via voice and video technology and meeting face to face at least once a month. This arrangement allows each participant to leverage its unique skills, for instance, protein expression at D10 or computational modeling at G10. G10 provides an annual grant to D10 and pays for all out-of-pocket reagents, travel expenses, and communication costs. Operating decisions are made jointly and each side contributes whatever manpower is required to fulfill the project plan, which is developed dynamically by the JPT.

Building a Successful Joint Endeavor

The defining characteristic of all joint endeavors is that both parties are heavily involved in the day-to-day work and operational decision making, as well as in governance and planning. The three variants differ according to when and how much the parties interact with each other.

An important prerequisite for success in all three variants is an effective and efficient mechanism for communicating complex information and insights between the two parties—not just concerning the data readouts and their interpretations, but also about how things were done, what options were considered, why certain decisions were made, what the dead ends were, what the alternative paths forward could be, and so on. This communication needs to happen at frequent and regular intervals in the pass-the-baton and divide-and-conquer variants, and on a weekly or even daily basis in the co-creative variant.

Dos and Don'ts of Partnership Models

When trying to determine the best model for your partnership, you need to focus on the essentials and clearly define each partner's needs. Starting from the models and variants described here, you can develop a customized partnership model and agreement by considering these questions in sequence:

a) What do both sides want to achieve?
b) What does each side bring to the table and how should it contribute?
c) Given the responses to the first two questions, what is the best way to conduct operations and make decisions?
d) What financial mechanisms and contractual agreements would best facilitate the above?

Beware of stereotyping partners. Not all academic research groups prefer hands-off sponsored R&D programs. The starting point for collaborating with a small IP-rich biotech is not necessarily wholesale IP transfer. While CROs are technically suppliers, it might make more sense to operate a risk-sharing drug discovery collaboration as a sponsored R&D program or joint endeavor.

Beware, too, of being sidetracked or confused by nomenclature. Just because the press release refers to a "joint venture agreement" does not mean both parties are jointly responsible for all operations and all decision making. In the same vein, just because the contract refers to a "licensing agreement" does not mean that the majority of what happens in the collaboration relates to the transfer of previously created intellectual property. Similarly "co-development" could mean both sides doing it together, or, at the other extreme, that one side pays for the other to do all the work.

It is absolutely essential that both parties develop a shared understanding of the partnership model that will govern the collaboration, regardless of what it is called, or even what it says or does not say in the signed contract. A common pitfall arises when one party has an implicit view, based on its past collaborations, of how the partnership should operate and assumes that the partner thinks in the same way. This can lead to any number of misunderstandings; for instance:

- A co-development collaboration between a multinational pharma and an established mid-sized biotech is viewed by the pharma as a project that will be conducted by its own R&D operation under its normal modus operandi with the biotech participating only as an essentially passive partner doing what it's told. The biotech is expecting an equal say in the decision making and wants its people to be closely involved so as to learn from the experience.
- A clinical trial conducted by a CRO is viewed by the pharma sponsor as a commodity purchase: "We know precisely what we want and we're tendering for the best price and the fastest execution." But the CRO sees it much more as a value-added collaborative exercise: "A lot of detailed design decisions are necessary and some practical compromises need to be made in order to meet the time-line expectations. Through collaborative thinking with our customer, we can bring to bear our previous experiences in this therapeutic area and our relationships with potential clinical investigators."
- An IP licensing agreement is viewed by the licensee as a one-time transfer of know-how, but the licensor sees an ongoing collaboration in which it needs to stay involved to ensure its IP has maximum impact and to capture important learnings on how the IP is applied practically.

These situations are especially common, and especially dangerous, with two parties who are new to each other. At best, this miscommunication can lead to confusion and wasted efforts until the parties align their perspectives through trial and error. At worst, it can lead to tension, distrust, and serious arguments, which could even derail the collaboration completely.

Pharma companies, under pressure from healthcare payers, seek ground-breaking new drugs that far surpass the performance of existing generic treatment options. As a consequence, there is a growing trend to increase creativity and engender more innovation in biopharma R&D collaborations. Such a requirement tends to favor partnership models that incorporate a high degree of interaction—the resulting creative tension is expected to lead to more innovative outcomes. Not surprisingly, we increasingly see more partnerships along the lines of those variants with higher levels of interaction.

Chapter Notes

[1] As we defined it in Chapter 1, *partnership* comprises arrangements between parties working collaboratively to allocate and share resources, operating responsibilities, decision making, benefits, and risks, regardless of whether such arrangements have been set out in a formal contract.

Chapter 5
Archetypes of Collaborating Organizations

The nature of any partnership will depend on the motivations, priorities, and constraints of the collaborators. In the biopharma world, the potential collaborators come from a wide variety of organizations, each with its own defining characteristics and particular needs. Understanding potential collaborators and their behavioral drivers is a key first step in constructing a productive, efficient and collegial partnership.

In this chapter, we look at the primary actors in the biopharma R&D ecosystem for innovative new medicines (Figure 5.1). Over the past 10–15 years, the most prevalent collaborators in private-funded bilateral partnerships, accounting for the vast majority of deals, have been multinational pharma marketers, academic investigators, research-stage biotech companies, focused biopharma companies, and R&D service providers. Consequently we focus in this chapter on archetypes of these five actors; the discussion of nonprofit R&D organizations, an emerging trend, is postponed to Chapter 11. For each archetype described in this chapter, we look at its:

- Strategic aims and business model;
- Rationale for R&D partnerships;
- Key stakeholders and internal processes; and
- Values, culture, and other drivers that impact its behavior in partnerships.

***Figure 5.1.* Key Actors and Influencers in the Biopharma R&D Ecosystem**

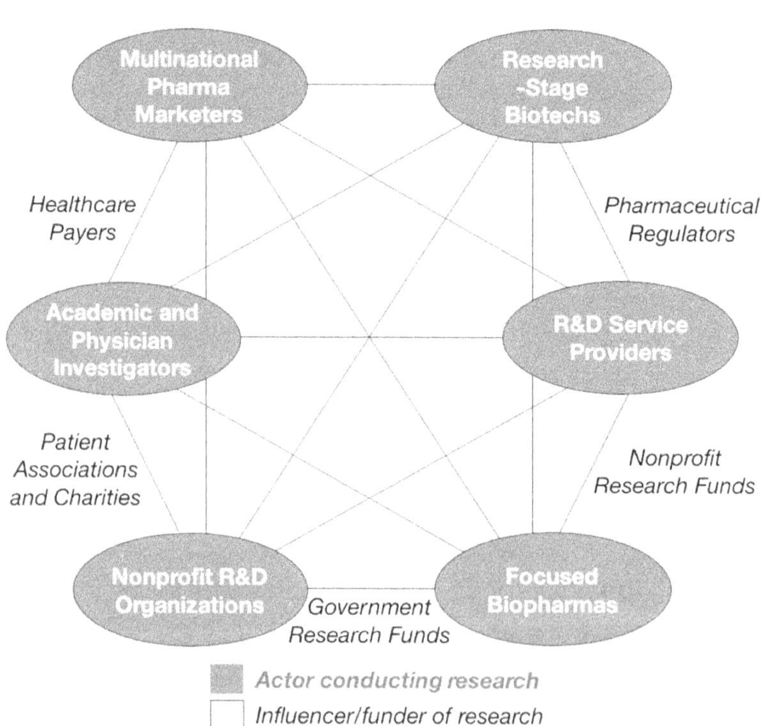

The aim in this discussion is to help you acquire a better understanding of current and potential partners and what drives their behavior, some aspects of which might initially appear counterintuitive. If you are comparatively new to biopharma R&D, or have worked primarily in only one type of organization, you may find these archetypes a useful primer on other types of organizations. They also provide a useful shorthand for use in later discussions.

Multinational Pharma Marketers

Multinational pharmaceutical corporations represent the classic Goliath in David & Goliath R&D partnerships. They are fully integrated companies whose primary business is marketing drugs across multiple countries via their own dedicated sales forces. Since they own the requisite MAs for their products, they are held accountable for pharmacovigilance by the regulatory authorities in each local geographic market that they choose to operate in. They have historically manufactured their products in-house, although most have now greatly increased the outsourcing of their physical supply chain activities to contract manufacturing organizations (CMOs).

While they often have substantial internal R&D organizations, multinational pharma marketers are very active in R&D collaborations and outsourcing. They fund and direct late-stage Phase III clinical trials and subsequent NDAs required to gain MAs. They also fund and direct post-approval Phase IV clinical programs, both to generate competitive data for marketing purposes and to comply with post-approval clinical study requirements mandated by regulatory authorities.

There are three distinct categories of multinational pharma marketers, each with somewhat different characteristics:

- Big pharmas.
- Mini-big pharmas.
- Mixed-model pharma marketers.

Big Pharmas

Big pharmas account for the lion's share of the private-sector funding pouring into the biopharma R&D ecosystem and are by far the most prevalent and active Goliaths in the arena of David & Goliath R&D partnerships. These companies, the very largest global pharma corporations, are huge, generating in excess of US$10 billion each in annual pharmaceutical sales; in 2014, this group comprised 22 firms (Figure 5.2). Some of these firms include other healthcare sectors in their business portfolios, such as medical devices (J&J), medical diagnostics (Roche), consumer health (Novartis, Bayer, and others), or vaccines (GSK, Sanofi). Companies such as Novartis, Teva, and Actavis are also global leaders in generic drugs through dedicated subsidiaries; others, like AbbVie and Eli Lilly, focus solely on patent-protected medicines. Many of the big pharmas have technology roots in traditional chemically-synthesized **small molecule drugs**, while a few, such as Amgen, made their names originally in biologically-manufactured protein drugs and continue to style themselves as biotech companies. In any case, most big pharmas have now embraced both small molecule drugs and **biologics** in their portfolio of R&D projects and marketed products.

Figure 5.2. **Largest Big Pharmas in 2014 (by global pharmaceutical sales, in million US$)**

1	Novartis	47,101
2	Pfizer	45,708
3	Roche	39,120
4	Sanofi	36,437
5	Merck & Co.	36,042
6	Johnson & Johnson (J&J)	32,313
7	GlaxoSmithKline (GSK)	29,580
8	AstraZeneca	26,095
9	Gilead	24,474
10	Takeda	20,446
11	AbbVie	20,207
12	Amgen	19,327
13	Teva	18,374
14	Eli Lilly	17,266
15	Bristol-Myers Squibb (BMS)	15,879
16	Bayer	15,486
17	Novo Nordisk	15,329
18	Astellas	14,099
19	Boehringer Ingelheim	13,830
20	Actavis	13,062
21	Otsuka	11,308
22	Daiichi Sankyo	10,430

Source: http://www.pmlive.com/top_pharma_list/global_revenues

Other than a few exceptions that are privately-owned such as Boehringer Ingelheim, the majority of big pharmas are accountable to a broad ownership base, with their shares freely traded on the world's capital markets. As such, they tend to have financially oriented strategic plans that aim to deliver against targeted financial performance metrics. At the corporate level, their business strategies prioritize resource allocation to defined therapeutic areas and healthcare sectors. The therapeutic area focus also aligns well with the way their sales forces are organized to engage with different kinds of physicians. Over the past ten to fifteen years, many big pharmas have faced steep **patent cliffs**, sharp drop-offs in revenues due to the expiration of patents—and ensuing competition from generics—on their blockbuster products. As a result, they have been forced to optimize operational costs and reduce overhead in order to meet financial targets. This necessity drove the companies to outsource operations and **off-shore** facilities to lower-cost countries.

The drive to reduce costs led to a significant rise in outsourced R&D operations via preferred provider partnerships with CROs in clinical, preclinical, and research areas, and with contract development and manufacturing organizations (CDMOs) in manufacturing process research and scale-up. That said, the primary driver of the tremendous growth in R&D externalization and the proliferation of David & Goliath R&D partnerships has been the severe, long-term decline of innovation and R&D productivity.

Owing to the scale and breadth of their business, big pharmas need to operate multidimensional matrix organization structures. Many managers have more than one boss to whom they must justify their decisions or from whom they must seek resources. These structures are often not static over a sustained period; the drive to become leaner over the past two decades has spawned successive waves of reorganization every few years. At the same time, high-potential managers are regularly assigned new roles as part of their professional development, so that a team may change regularly even if the organizational framework is stable.

As a result of these economic and organizational dynamics, in a David & Goliath partnership, David's comparatively small team has to work with a confusing multitude of big pharma people from therapeutic area groups, business development functions, regulatory, legal, project management, alliance management, and a range of technical R&D functions (depending on the area and scope of the collaboration), including clinical operations, medical affairs, toxicology, ADME, and so forth. Furthermore, the big pharma's collaboration team members are likely to be based across several different geographical locations and time zones. Compounding the difficulty, the frequency of reorganizations and personnel reshufflings forces David to continually build relationships with new people.

David also has to live with the big pharmas' seemingly complex processes for business development, due diligence, and contracting at the outset of the collaboration, and subsequently during execution for project budgeting, review, steering, and portfolio management. The deliberations and decision criteria in these processes are neither fully transparent nor intuitive to David, especially given that David cannot be privy to confidential information originating in the large company's other internal projects and external collaborations. A classic example is the collaboration that is put on hold or canceled in the big pharma's portfolio management review even though its scientific progress seemed perfectly satisfactory from David's perspective.

From the big pharma perspective, executives understand that biopharma R&D is a game of low success probabilities and progressively higher investments. In this context, it makes perfect sense to deliberately initiate, for example, ten research collaborations in a particular therapeutic area with the intention of initiating clinical trials in only five and eventually taking only one or two to market. Rather than making decisions on the basis of the absolute best science or the most pressing medical needs, big pharmas make decisions intended to deliver on business strategies and financial targets within their resource constraints. The individual performance objectives and incentives of big pharma executives and managers have been designed to reinforce this approach.

It is tempting for David to decry its big pharma partner's bureaucracy, complexity, and culture, but Davids need to recognize that these characteristics are an unavoidable consequence of the big pharma's scale, depth of resources, and global reach—the very attributes that Davids benefit from in a partnership.

Mini-Big Pharmas

The **mini-big pharmas** are smaller than the big pharmas but have similar business models and approaches; these companies typically have annual sales (in 2015 dollars) of US$2 billion to US$8 billion (in contrast to the big pharmas, which each generate in excess of US$10 billion). At the time of writing, examples of mini-big pharmas include Celgene, Eisai, Kyowa Hakko Kirin, Merck Serono (known as EMD Serono in North America), Menarini, Mylan, Servier, Shire, and UCB, among others. Like the big pharmas, the mini-big pharmas operate globally and control a complete value chain, from research to manufacturing and sales; they are listed on the world's capital markets and depend on pharmaceuticals as their primary driver of shareholder value growth. They are more focused in their business strategies than their larger brethren, concentrating on a smaller number of therapeutic areas or other focused domains, such as specialist medicines, orphan diseases, emerging economies, **biosimilars**, or generic drugs. In their fields of specialty, they can and do go head-to-head with the big pharmas.

As they are more compact in size than the big pharmas, mini-big pharmas operate with a less complex organization, one with fewer management layers that enables more nimble decision making. Like the big pharmas, most are very active in external R&D collaborations, usually playing the Goliath role in David & Goliath partnerships. In my interviews with the leaders of David organizations, many of these leaders identified a mini-big pharma company as the Goliath partner they most enjoyed working with, usually mentioning that their mini-big pharma partners had exhibited greater flexibility, more entrepreneurial thinking, greater openness, and a more human touch compared to the big pharmas—an unsurprising cultural legacy given that as recently as two decades ago most of these companies were either family businesses, entrepreneurial spinoffs, or smaller biotech firms.

Mixed-Model Pharma Marketers

Outside the top fifty or so largest pharmaceutical companies, there are perhaps another forty to sixty companies worldwide who operate as smaller **mixed-model pharma marketers**. They operate internationally, generating roughly (in 2015 dollars) US$500 million to US$2 billion in annual revenues from sales of pharmaceutical products plus a mixed bag of related revenue sources that comprise some combination of proprietary drugs, generic drugs, drug delivery systems, APIs, consumer health, fine chemicals, medical diagnostics, contract finished dose manufacturing, royalties, and R&D partnerships. Many of these companies have roots as national or regional pharmaceutical marketing companies; this category includes (at the time of writing) Esteve, Gedeon Richter, and Orion Pharma in Europe, as well as many of the larger Indian and smaller Japanese companies. As a result, these companies tend to have a regional focus in their marketing activities and R&D operations. Some have aspirations to become mini-big pharmas, while others are content to deliver steady growth for their owners.

Most of these companies conduct some R&D in-house and are active in external R&D collaborations as either a David, a Goliath, or a peer partner. They often operate quite entrepreneurially, with a nimble and flexible business approach that is appreciated by collaborating partners. Such companies typically have a small number of controlling owners who have a long-term perspective, and they often have only a few key decision makers in their management hierarchy. This allows them to make quick decisions, but they are also very picky about the nature and scope of the partnerships they enter into. They have tight resource constraints and limited capacity to manage more than a few major initiatives beyond their daily business. And they are more risk averse than the larger companies, hence the balanced mix of revenue sources. However, some are adapting their business models to proactively embrace the rapid growth in R&D externalization across the biopharma sector.

Academic Investigators

The academic research group is a classic David.[1] The typical academic bioscience research group (often called a laboratory) is led by a senior academic (the **principal investigator**, PI) who is ultimately responsible for the group's focus and for ensuring sufficient funding for the laboratory's activities. The remainder of the group comprises postdocs, PhD students, laboratory technicians, and administrative support staff. This group could stand on its own, although it is more typically part of a larger unit of related groups. For example, the Center for Molecular Medicine at Sweden's renowned Karolinska Institutet comprises 38 research groups spread across its four focus areas of cardiovascular and metabolic diseases, inflammation, genetic diseases, and neurogenetics and psychiatric diseases.

The need to publish is the primary behavioral driver in an academic research group; the "publish or perish" imperative is a reality for most academic researchers. A closely related second imperative is the need to secure funding for the group; the laboratory head and senior postdocs spend much of their time writing grant applications. The two drives are related—many grant providers are public-sector or nonprofit entities who use publications as important criteria for determining awards, measured not just by volume but also by the reputational ranking of the journals in which a researcher is published and by the number of citations back to a researcher's published work.

On an individual level, academics like challenging and interesting work that has the potential to generate the high-quality publications that power academic advancement and recognition. Historically, many industry-academic collaborations have taken the form of the industry sponsor treating the academic laboratory as a CRO to conduct piecemeal studies and experiments to order, using specialist models, tools, or biological samples that the laboratory has unique access to. These unique tools were often the principal reasons the sponsor found the collaboration attractive. However, academics see such arrangements as repetitive and boring, and unlikely to advance their research careers. A big pharma alliance manager described the academic mindset to me:

> The principal investigator may like the money, but the lab staff, many of them highly rated postdocs in their field, hate being treated like production workers ... unless you can make it intellectually interesting for them! Otherwise, the best you can reasonably expect in these situations is that they execute the work within the terms of the contract, with much of the repetitive work actually carried out by comparatively inexperienced doctoral or even master's students.

Academic researchers and industry sponsors may also clash over the timing of publications. The academic researcher wants to publish findings as quickly as possible, to stay ahead of academic competitors, but the typical industry sponsor would rather competitors know as little and as late as possible what results its research is generating. For this reason, industry-academic collaborations have historically focused on basic research, such as disease etiology, or precompetitive domains, such as disease biomarkers or predictive toxicology tools.

The handling of IP can also be an issue in industry-academic partnerships. Increasingly, university technology transfer offices and some individual researchers have become very proactive in protecting the IP emerging from the academic research, often creating spin-off corporate entities to hold and exploit it. This is especially true in North America and the United Kingdom. Interestingly, some biopharmas see this development as a good thing because it creates a more commercially oriented relationship when they collaborate. However, other companies are less positive about this development, having found that academic researchers often greatly underestimate the distance, risk, and costs to be navigated before an experimental molecule ever reaches the market, and hence tend to greatly overvalue their IP.

As a result of these mismatched priorities, alignment between industry and academia is inherently difficult. Besides the pragmatic needs to publish and to secure funding, the emotional motivation of many academics is the intellectual challenge, and for those in basic bioscience research especially, the truth-seeking activity of discovering why the workings of the human body are the way they are. Only a small minority of academics are driven by industry's mission of creating commercially viable products—and even this minority often do not understand the pharmaceutical R&D process and or why IP protection and regulatory requirements mandate rigorously documented laboratory notes, experimental protocols, and process guidelines. Furthermore, it is much harder to enforce contractual deliverables and timelines in the more loosely controlled academic environment, even if the group's leader is supportive.

However, these challenges are not insurmountable, especially if both the biopharma sponsors and the academic laboratory heads work to find ways to ensure that the whole academic team has the motivation and desire to deliver what the sponsor needs, and that the industry sponsor provides at least some of the primary academic motivators. For instance, even as more collaborations go further into the drug discovery domain, an increasing number of partnerships manage their scope to ensure that the academic group has the potential to publish interesting papers.

Academics may also be motivated by other incentives, such as access to scientific tools, hard-to-source reagents, specialist equipment, and other items that support their research interests. Sponsors who provide this type of in-kind support are typically highly appreciated. Sponsors can also deploy some of their own people to transfer or develop new assays for the academic team to use, or to conduct experiments on specialist in-house equipment on behalf of the academics. This kind of interaction has the additional benefits of building the relationship and creating opportunities for valuable new insights to emerge.

As with any collaboration, personal chemistry and stable relationships are highly valued. Many academics have become wary of companies constantly restructuring their organizations, which some feel has led to a loss of know-how. Academic researchers respect a sensible and interesting dialogue about the results from their work and expect that sponsors will have a critical mass of know-how in the relevant scientific domains. As I was told by the head of an academic laboratory:

> We hate the musical chairs every two to three years from reorganizations and mergers. Some of the big pharmas are hollowing out their scientific expertise; increasingly they can't judge good versus bad, and struggle to have meaningful scientific dialogue in very specialist areas.

Academics also look at a prospective sponsor's reputation for integrity and its track record for treating academia fairly and with respect. When approached by a company they have not worked with before, most academics will reach out to their network to ask about their peers' experiences with the company. The company's public reputation is important too, especially with regard to any negative publicity concerning ethical behavior.

Given the need to build relationships and establish trust, biopharma companies may find it helpful to develop a bridge to academic organizations step by step. For example, a new collaboration could start with comparatively low-cost (but high-profile) funding of a few postdocs and PhD students, which would give the company the chance to build trust, mutual understanding, and an awareness of the corporate brand. From there, the company could move to projects with more senior researchers and laboratory heads.

Research-Stage Biotech Companies

In thinking about David & Goliath R&D partnerships, the classic David many people have in mind is the **research-stage biotech company**, spun out from an academic research lab or a larger business and funded by venture capital investors to exploit an initial IP package. Cash flow, IP, and enterprise valuation are the things that matter most to such companies, the money being needed to apply and extend the IP, eventually leading to the creation of valuable scientific assets. R&D partnerships with larger organizations are the lifeblood of such organizations, for two closely related reasons:

- Partnerships bring in funding and expertise from external collaboration partners.
- Partnerships facilitate investor financing by boosting the confidence of existing investors while building the company's credibility and attractiveness to new investors.

The culture in research-stage biotechs tends to be collaborative, energetic, and can-do, and their people are in principle very open to engaging with external partners. However, external engagements sometimes bring a rude awakening to these companies and their personnel, especially for first-timers—many are not prepared for the scale of the differences in the culture and business approach of their Goliath partner. This is particularly the case for scientists who have come from an academic or small company background and have not been exposed to the organizational and process complexity of the typical Goliath partner.

Because they rely on external investment to fund IP development, research-stage biotechs have a strong need for frequent news flow—a constant stream of new information that reassures investors as well as current and prospective partners that what they have is unique, effective, and ultimately valuable. In their search for the most financially attractive deals with the most newsworthy external partners, these companies sometimes engage in partnerships that may not represent the best choices for the longer-term health of the company. For example, a deal with a rich and famous big pharma that provides sorely needed short-term funding and investor kudos will be prioritized over what could be a much more valuable, long-term partnership with a cash-poor, low-profile focused biopharma that has unique expertise related to the research-stage biotech's scientific assets. In a similar vein, biotech management teams and their controlling investors sometimes opt for partnerships in therapeutic areas or indications where they have lower chances of success because those areas have a large potential market size and consequent impact on enterprise valuation. By doing so, they may eschew partnerships with much higher likelihoods of success, albeit in areas with smaller expected commercial returns.

A primary strategic concern for investors in research-stage biotechs is finding viable paths to an attractive exit. They need to capture a high return on their investment, either by selling their ownership to another party or by converting their stake into publicly tradable securities on the world's capital markets. Typically, the company will have successive waves of investors as it develops and its scientific assets move closer to becoming marketed products. In recent years, we have seen increased activity in this arena by big pharma venture capital subsidiaries; for these investors, the investment offers the additional carrot of the potential that their stake could eventually be converted into a partnership or even an outright acquisition.

These early-stage companies are constantly hungry for funding and keen to keep their fixed costs down. A model currently popular with startup biotech investors is the **asset-centric company**. In this approach, there is no attempt to establish a long-term business. Instead the aim is to develop the initial IP as quickly as possible and demonstrate its value through exciting experimental results, with the aim to sell the whole company to a bigger R&D player for a substantial return on investment. Asset-centric companies tend to be very lean and often do not have laboratory facilities of their own, conducting most of their R&D operations via CROs. The few dedicated employees typically comprise the chief executive, a few scientific leaders, and finance and business development specialists. There are even management teams who look after several asset-centric companies concurrently. Such an approach suits both classic venture investors and also the venture arms of the big pharmas, who appreciate that, in the event of a partnership or acquisition, they need not worry about integrating large numbers of people and physical facilities.

As funding is hard to come by in the early days, some research-stage biotechs generate cash flow by operating as **specialist CROs**, using the company's IP and skills to provide unique services to other players in the biopharma R&D space. If the IP can be developed and packaged into a patented technology platform that enables therapeutic or diagnostic applications, that platform can be licensed to other R&D organizations for use in their own projects. Typically, the R&D partnership deals struck by such technology providers include some combination of license royalties and service provision fees.

Although there are many startup and small research-stage biotechs operating one or both of these two business models to pay the bills, neither is a stable arrangement; these structures are usually transitory, persisting only until the company can be sold or some more stable source of funding can be accessed. Indeed, research-stage biotechs are rarely static. They either go bankrupt, get acquired, or evolve into something else. To become an established research-stage biotech, the company must achieve critical mass and grow into an **asset-generating engine** that consistently creates scientific assets at key value inflection points. For these companies, the business model is based on selling these assets or leveraging them via partnerships with larger companies that in turn take them to the next stages and eventually into marketed products.

An asset-generating engine can evolve into a **product company**—that is, one that takes its (at least 50%-owned) projects through late-stage development to product registration, partnering with other companies for worldwide commercialization. If the product's indication requires a relatively small, focused sales force, the company may also become a **specialty marketer**, operating in a few geographic markets while partnering with others to access markets in the rest of the world. If either of these two states is achieved, the company has transitioned to become a focused biopharma company.

Focused Biopharmas

Now we come to a particularly interesting species that is flourishing in the rapidly evolving biopharma R&D ecosystem. **Focused biopharmas** come in a number of varieties. Some have strong revenue flows from marketed products and can be as large as the smaller mixed-model pharmas. Others have products only at the late-development stage and rely on funding from investors and partnerships. Whatever the company's structure and business model, however, focused biopharmas all share four characteristics that distinguish them from the other archetypes:

- They have achieved critical mass and as such are established companies with secure balance sheets and revenue streams, even if they might currently be operating at a loss. Unlike the research-stage biotechs, they are usually not overly concerned about near-term survival.
- They adopt distinctive business models unique to their individual circumstances, usually defined by combining certain scientific or functional specialties with a specific value chain focus. They choose, as an integral part of their strategy, to focus their internal operations and strengthen their capabilities in specific parts of the pharmaceutical value chain, relying on collaborations and strategic outsourcing for the rest. In contrast, the multinational pharma marketer archetypes tend to operate a complete value chain (albeit with a certain degree of outsourcing) and define their strategy by the therapeutic areas and business sectors in which they operate.
- They may or may not have their own sales forces, but their business culture reflects a history as a research, development, or technically focused company, unlike the pharma marketer archetypes, which tend to have a more commercially dominated business culture.
- They tend to have proactive owners who see a significant long-term upside in their companies' enterprise valuations and employ growth-oriented management teams to invest and build the organization over a sustained period. Many similar-sized pharma marketers are more risk-averse mature businesses that view preservation of value and reliable profit generation as a critical consideration. In contrast, although the owners of small research-stage biotechs may also see a big upside in maximizing value,

they are more likely to be looking for a transformative deal or sale of the company in the short to medium term.

Some focused biopharmas, such as (at time of writing in mid-2015) Actelion, Alexion, and Regeneron, started out as research-stage biotechs seeking to discover and develop new medicines, often based on assets spun off from academic research or bigger companies. Over time, such firms, with the support of their investors and collaboration partners, managed to avoid being acquired and launched their own products, building sustainable revenue streams in the process.

A focused biopharma can also emerge from an old school mixed-model pharma marketer. For example, the Swiss company Helsinn has (at time of writing) transformed itself over the past decade and a half from its roots as an API producer and regional pharma marketer into a global drug developer and licensor, North American specialty pharma marketer, and consumer health product company, with all of these business elements focused on the common theme of cancer supportive care. Helsinn's operating model is a good illustration of the specific value chain focus typical of focused biopharmas. The company has built strong in-house capabilities in business development, clinical management, regulatory, project leadership, strategic marketing, and product management while relying on collaboration and outsourcing partners for new compounds, preclinical testing, clinical operations, and local sales promotion, among other things.

Not every focused biopharma needs to deploy a global sales force to be successful and sustainable. A focused development company like Debiopharm or Helsinn typically operates by acquiring or in-licensing compounds at the candidate drug or first-in-man inflection points. It then develops these assets for a range of target indications and geographies in its therapy areas of interest until submission (NDA) or regulatory approval (MA) before partnering with commercial collaborators to market the resulting products.

By design, the business model of most focused biopharmas relies heavily on David & Goliath collaborations in both the R&D and commercial arenas. If they have products that have reached the market, they rely on Goliath (and sometimes even David) collaborators for marketing and sales. In R&D, they are very active as Goliath partners with academic researchers, research-stage biotech firms, and smaller CROs, and as David partners with big pharmas, mini-big pharmas, and large multinational CROs. Focused biopharmas tend to be nimble and entrepreneurial, with comparatively few management layers and prompt decision making. As Goliath, they can be more sympathetic to the needs of their David collaborators since they also live in David roles with other partners, but they have fewer resources and in-house capabilities to draw upon compared to larger pharmas. As David, they come across to their partners as less emotional in their decision making than research-stage biotechs and academic partners, while having a broader experience base and more tested scientific capabilities.

R&D Service Providers

Contrary to popular belief, **R&D service providers**, or CROs, are not merely commodity outsourcing companies that do things companies could otherwise have done in-house, and using a CRO is not always about avoiding fixed costs. In a lot of cases, CROs can do certain things faster, cheaper, and to a higher standard because they have more experience in both the execution and the interpretation of specific tasks. Experienced CRO personnel can also be good collaborators in designing and planning scientific work, not just achieving cost and speed benefits but also extracting more or better information from the work done.

Most CROs start life either as research-stage biotechs coming out of academic environments or as spin-outs from larger pharma and biotech companies. The aggressive organizational restructuring and downsizing of the big pharmas over the past decade has created many new CROs. Not all of these pharma spin-outs survive after the flow of work that is guaranteed as part of the separation transaction runs out, especially if they do not offer anything better than or different from what is already out there. At the same time, however, those CROs that can improve on others' offerings, or provide unique inputs, are growing rapidly on the back of the move toward R&D externalization.

Broadly speaking, there are three different segments of service providers in biopharma R&D:

- ***Clinical CROs*** provide services related to clinical trials, including protocol design, patient recruitment, trial monitoring, sample analysis, data management, biostatistics, medical writing, and regulatory advice, much of this activity conducted within the Good Clinical Practice (GCP) guidelines mandated by regulatory authorities.
- ***Nonclinical CROs*** provide services related to *in vitro* and *in vivo* experimental studies. Some of these companies maintain expensive facilities that operate according to the GLP guidelines required for the preclinical toxicology studies that preface the first clinical studies for a candidate drug. Other nonclinical CROs operate earlier in the value chain, supporting the drug discovery and disease research stages where GLP-standard facilities are not required.
- ***Chemical manufacturing and control (CMC)*** service providers support the design, development, and scale-up of manufacturing processes for both APIs (also referred to as **drug substances**) and the FDF (also referred to as the **drug product** or **galenic form**). CMC refers to the section of the FDA's new drug application that relates to manufacturing processes. CMC service providers usually have to conduct

some aspects of their work subject to Good Manufacturing Practice (GMP) guidelines and are often part of larger CDMOs that not only help their customers develop manufacturing processes but also produce the resulting APIs and FDFs once the product reaches the market.

There is a crossover area between the production and distribution of supplies for clinical trials. Technically speaking, such functions would be CMC activities, since they require manufacturing under GLP and GMP the substances that will be tested in clinical trials. However, some clinical and nonclinical CROs also include these services in their portfolios.

Some CROs combine segments, offering services across functions; Aptuit, for example, provides both nonclinical and CMC services. There is also an increasing number of medium-sized companies operating a hybrid model, in which they operate both as nonclinical CROs and as discovery-focused biopharmas; companies operating in this way include (at time of writing in mid-2015) Evotec in Europe, Aurigene in India, and Hutchison Medi Pharma in China.

The large multinational CROs, such as Charles River Laboratories (nonclinical), Quintiles (clinical), and Catalent (CMC/CDMO), tend to be listed on the capital markets, and as such have shareholder expectations for financial results and growth that they need to meet. Typically, they seek to grow by adding new customer accounts, broadening their range of services, and increasing account penetration (selling more to existing customers) via a combination of organic development and acquisition of smaller CROs. Within the segments and subsegments in which they have chosen to compete, they aim to provide a full range of services, functioning as a one-stop shop for their customers.

In addition to investing in their technical capabilities, large CROs have built up highly professional business development and customer account management teams and regularly conduct initiatives to optimize their processes and use of information technology. However, they are increasingly struggling to differentiate themselves from each other. Most have gone down the route of developing preferred provider partnerships in which they seek to integrate their processes closely with their customers' R&D operations. Some have also implemented performance-based pricing arrangements and risk-reward-sharing deals in a bid to grow margins. And many are driving CRO industry consolidation through aggressive acquisition programs intended to grow both their top and bottom lines.

Among smaller to medium-sized CROs, there is a much greater diversity of ownership, ambitions, strategy, and culture. Some of these companies are listed on the capital markets or owned by professional private equity investors and are essentially seeking to become large multinational players by mimicking the strategies of the larger companies. At the other extreme, there are lifestyle businesses, owned by their management teams or a small group of family members whose primary aim is to ensure a steady income for everyone involved in the business.

New CROs spun out from pharma companies must decide early on whether to be growth business or lifestyle businesses. If growth is the object, new investors probably need to be found to inject fresh capital to fund both organic growth and acquisitions. In that case, the end game—several years hence—is either to sell the company to a bigger CRO or to list it on the capital markets. Even if the choice is to be a lifestyle business, a certain amount of growth may still be needed, to increase scale (so as to remain price competitive) and to broaden the customer base and service portfolio so that the business is resilient to longer-term changes in the business cycle and new technology developments.

Another key choice facing a smaller to medium-sized CRO is the nature of its customer proposition along two key dimensions:

- Should it offer a broad range or a focused set of services?

- Will these services be essentially undifferentiated (providing a commodity service) or will the company seek to add significant customer-specific value in the service design or delivery or both?

For smaller specialist CROs with unique skills that can create distinctive IP, there is also the option of following some of the same paths available to research-stage biotechs.

The multinational CROs know how to work with multinational pharma marketers, as many of their organizational behavioral drivers are not that dissimilar. Similarly, the smaller CROs often collaborate easily with research-stage biotechs, focused biopharmas, and academia, with whom they share similar management approaches and orientations. Small CROs face the same challenges as research-stage biotechs when dealing with the larger pharmas, and the David-perspective discussions in this book apply equally to them. An intriguing case arises when academic researchers, research-stage biotechs, and focused biopharmas work with large multinational CROs, creating a curious reversal of the usual roles in which the CRO is the Goliath and the customer is the David.

Applying the Archetypes

These archetypes illustrate the diverse concerns and issues that may be in play in any partnership. Indeed, individual organizations will have specific characteristics beyond those mentioned in these general profiles. Understanding what organizational factors are in play is critical to structuring and executing a successful collaboration. David personnel, in particular, may feel powerless before what seem to be mysterious and unpredictable decision-making processes in large multinational corporations, whether these be pharmas or CROs. Grasping the forces driving such decisions will help small players navigate the challenges of collaboration and negotiate better outcomes for their collaborative partnerships.

Chapter Notes

[1] In this section, we discuss academic researchers as collaborators within the traditional industry-academic collaborative setting of sponsored research programs. In Chapter 11, we will explore the more recent phenomenon of academic researchers being closely integrated into industry R&D projects and of nonprofit organizations initiating and driving such projects themselves. For simplicity of exposition, we use here the language of early-stage disease research and drug discovery, but similar comments also apply to physician investigators involved in later-stage clinical trials, as well as to academic researchers in areas such as clinical trials, drug delivery, and galenic formulation.

Part B: Improving the Odds

Part B dives into the practical aspects of bilateral David & Goliath R&D partnerships, looking at what can be done at different stages of the partnership to improve the odds of beneficial partnership outcomes. Over these four chapters, we will walk through the life cycle of a partnership (see Figure B.1), discussing the key issues and opportunities at each stage.

Figure B.1. Life Cycle of a Partnership

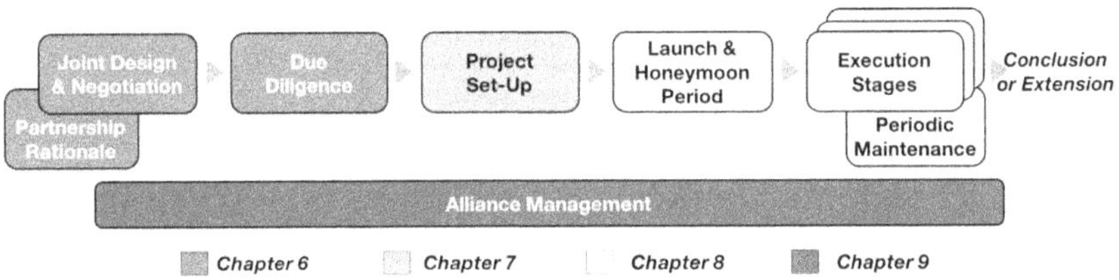

CHAPTER 6
PARTNERSHIP STRATEGY AND DESIGN

Pursuing a partnership can be a huge decision, particularly for a small or young organization. For David companies, it may be a strategic necessity. Whatever the motivator, partnerships should be approached thoughtfully, with an eye toward making sure that potential partners are a good fit, having complementary strategic goals and approaches and a culture that will support the project through development. Ensuring a successful collaboration begins with selecting the right partner and designing a partnership structure to support the collaboration through to its (hopefully successful) conclusion.

In this chapter, we consider how organizations triage prospective partnerships in the context of an overall partnering strategy and how partnerships can be designed and negotiated to meet both parties' goals. An important element in this process is due diligence; the final part of the chapter explores some common misconceptions and blind spots that can undermine the due diligence process, sometimes leading to uncomfortable surprises as the project moves forward.

This chapter uses language usually associated with sponsored R&D programs or joint R&D endeavors. However, the key concepts explicated here will also apply to value-added supply and IP transfer arrangements.

Evaluating the Strategic Fit of Prospective Partners and Partnerships

The first step in building a successful collaboration is choosing the right partner—one that has complementary strengths and goals, as well as useful skills and assets, in terms of both IP and facilities. In the bilateral David & Goliath partnership, David and Goliath will have very different criteria for evaluating prospective partnerships and assessing strategic fit.

Goliath's Partnership Rationale

In considering a new partnership, Goliath will be focused on how the prospective partner and project fit with its strategy for a given therapeutic area. Thus, Goliath's decision maker is usually the relevant therapeutic area leadership team. That team, in consultation with corporate management, will have defined in advance a therapeutic area strategy that prioritizes some combination of disease areas, unmet needs for specific diseases and indications, drug target classes, and technologies, all subject to resource constraints and prescribed timelines. Ideally, for Goliath, the projects addressing these priorities will fall at various stages of the R&D process. Any prospective partnership suggested by the business development or scouting organizations will be triaged for its fit with this comprehensive strategy.

Portfolio thinking is an integral component of most therapeutic area strategies for big pharma companies. This mindset shapes their partnering approach in two ways. First, external partnerships and internal projects are all part of the same portfolio. This means external partnerships will be considered only if they fill gaps in the internal portfolio, provide a better option than an existing internal project, or diversify overall portfolio risk. Second, the portfolio management process anticipates the industry's low R&D success rates by launching many more projects than will proceed through to the final stages. For external collaborations, this means that many early-stage projects will be accepted, but there is usually not enough funding to take all of them through to the later stages, even if they all achieve their aims. Rather, projects will be pruned throughout the development process until only the strongest remain. Even a partnership with a strong rationale at launch may find itself terminated at a later stage, as everything is looked at from a portfolio perspective—which may dictate decisions that appear, from outside, to be at odds with individual project results.

David's Partnership Rationale

David leadership teams, I have observed, typically take one of three distinct approaches in evaluating a potential partnership:

- Develop a *planned*, detailed partnering strategy with clear descriptors of acceptable deals up front, and then triage all prospective deals against those criteria.
- Be mostly *opportunistic*; any prospective deal appearing that is within the organization's broad scope is evaluated on its individual merits.
- Take a *hybrid* approach in which a high-level partnering plan is developed but decision makers are open to adjust-

ing this plan dynamically if an opportunity appears that is too good to pass up.

In theory, the planned approach is the most logical, but in practice it is the least effective, as many good opportunities cannot be foreseen—the temptation to become overly detailed, and thus overly restrictive—is nearly inescapable. Most decision-making teams that start with the first approach end up adopting the hybrid approach, whether they admit it or not. The opportunistic approach might seem the least rational, but it is what many David organizations start with, although they, too, often end up with the hybrid approach eventually. The hybrid approach is the most pragmatic, since it improves the chances of avoiding a catastrophic deal by focusing the search process while allowing for unforeseen possibilities. In any case, the other two approaches usually end up converging toward a hybrid model.

Some organizations do consciously choose the hybrid approach at the outset, and undertake clear steps to support it, first defining a partnering strategy and then implementing or adapting it as opportunities emerge. As a foundation for the partnering strategy, the David organization's leadership team must first consciously align itself on the organization's strategic aims—what does the team really want for the organization in the long term?

A high-level partnering strategy comprises two components: the corporate partnering strategy and the asset partnering strategy. The **corporate partnering strategy** describes the total portfolio of assets potentially available for partnering, sets out in broad terms the role each asset plays in the organization's long-term strategy, and prioritizes them for partnering. For those who have (and can generate more) protectable IP, each asset comprises a bundle of distinct IP, activities, and related in-house knowledge, skills, and tools. For example, a project to generate a candidate drug for an orphan indication could be one asset; its strategic role might be to support a goal to create a product that the company could market in North America with its own sales force. The liposome-based drug delivery technology developed to support that project could be split off as a separate technology platform asset that could serve as a cash generator by being licensed to as many different partners as possible.

For CROs and some academic groups that cannot or do not want to generate protectable IP, the asset is simply a package of related in-house knowledge, skills, and tools; for example, a set of services and corresponding tools to assess the safety profile of a prospective drug molecule could constitute a partnerable asset. Such an asset is not necessarily a commodity, since particular skills may be scarce and some tools—such as, for instance, an *ex vivo* assay based on a unique source of tissue samples—cannot be easily replicated. Even those companies that do generate protectable IP might find it worthwhile to define unprotected assets that can generate revenue via CRO-like arrangements.

The **asset partnering strategy**, which emerges from the corporate partnering strategy, defines preferred partnership models and prioritized partner archetypes for a particular shareable asset. The models and archetypes outlined in Chapters 4 and 5 could serve as templates for asset partnering strategies. For example, the partnering strategy for an anti-inflammatory candidate drug might read something like this:

- Partner should be a multinational pharma with a long-established franchise in inflammation-related diseases that has launched new, innovative products in the past decade.
- Partner must have skills in exploratory clinical development, including the translational tools to identify the most appropriate indication for the fastest route to market.
- The partnership model should be a form of joint endeavor in which the originating organization's people get to participate in (or at least shadow) the development of the clinical and commercial plans. It should not be a straight

IP transfer with no further involvement since the organization has a strategic aim to develop its own clinical and commercial capabilities.

- Financial terms must cover all the development costs including in-house costs for the project, so that the originating organization will not need to raise additional investor funding to take the molecule forward. Since the molecule is quite hard to make, the originator is willing to trade lower royalty rates on net revenues in exchange for a manufacturing contract at pre-defined terms fixed over a minimum multi-year duration.

When a partnering opportunity comes on the table for a shareable asset, the organization will assess it against the relevant asset partnering strategy. This assessment is conducted both by reviewing written materials and, if appropriate, by assigning a team to engage in preliminary discussions with the prospective partner. The opportunity may not be an exact match to the asset partnering strategy, but the strategy provides a baseline from which to negotiate, and having the strategy will help negotiators remain conscious of how far they are straying from that baseline if they elect to pursue the opportunity further. Negotiators and managers should have sufficient flexibility to adjust the asset partnering strategy when an opportunity brings to light certain features of an asset that were not anticipated or sufficiently understood in the original strategy, even if they end up not pursuing the specific deal that called attention to those features.

Furthermore, based on the experience of evaluating a number of asset partnering deals, whether consummated or otherwise, the corporate partnering strategy might then be adjusted periodically in the light of the lessons learnt.

Logic Traps and Pragmatic Compromises

The process of deciding whether to partner a particular asset or capability, and at what terms, can be difficult. The issues involved are complex, and decisions often must be made under significant time pressure. Still, it is important that decision makers take the time to identify and preempt logical traps that can result in poorly considered deals. Furthermore, decision makers need to avoid acting out of short-term expediency or based on knee-jerk reactions to unexpected circumstances. Take for example the leadership team of the research-stage biotech that "needs a deal soon" in order to support the next round of investor fund raising. With a number of partnering discussions in progress, that team could be sorely tempted to go with the project that has the shortest timeline and the highest probability of closure. Or consider a therapeutic area leadership team in a multinational pharma that has received poor results from a couple of its key projects, forcing those projects to be aborted. That team, under pressure to fill the hole in its pipeline as soon as possible, may be likely to jump on the next partnering proposal that can be justified, even if it does not fit that closely with the current portfolio or business strategy, rather than risk having funds reallocated to another therapeutic area.

Some research-stage biotechs or small specialist CROs will be drawn to the deal that generates the highest impact on the company's short-term enterprise valuation, neglecting alternatives that may have much greater longer-term benefit. In a similar vein, a trap that sometimes affects both Goliath and David organizations is jumping on the bandwagon of currently-fashionable scientific trends. Approaches that are in vogue generate published papers, attract attention from vocal scientific opinion leaders, and draw many big players to invest. Getting a deal signed in such a hot area can have a positive short-term impact on how both partners are perceived by their stakeholders. And it is usually quite easy to construct a compelling business case for such a trendy project, since the established wisdom will tend to generate very attractive financial forecasts. But history has proven that many of today's hot areas become tomorrow's dead ends. Even if the scientific basis does turn out to be solid, the Goliath pharma in question may not have the capabilities to exploit it better or faster than its competitors.

Having mentioned all of the above, sometimes there is not a lot of choice when all is said and done. "Needs must," as they say, and companies will occasionally take deals that are not ideal, the consequences of which they must manage afterwards. In such cases, the leadership team usually knows that the decision is probably not optimal in the medium to long term, but they make the choice anyway, because action is imperative and other alternatives are simply unacceptable. In the end, partnering is about doing a deal you can live with. The important thing in this case is to be consciously aware you are making this compromise.

Designing the Partnership

Once the David leadership team decides that a potential partnership is likely to have an acceptable strategic fit—or are offered other opportunities worth the divergence from the strategy—the next step is to ascertain the acceptability of the partnership from the financial, operational, and cultural points of view. In practice, it is impossible to fully evaluate these aspects without successive rounds of discussions and negotiations with the other party. In the process, the two teams—David's and Goliath's—develop the partnership model jointly, allowing both to get their arms around the operating and financial arrangements; the process of working with the other party to do so is in itself a test of the cultural fit.

The dialogue with the prospective partner usually starts with an informal, high-level exchange of views on:

- Each party's expected contribution, in terms of funding, IP, expertise, operations, and other elements.
- The likely nature of the legal transaction—asset sale, licensing deal, customized service contract, joint venture agreement, or other structure.
- The generally preferred mechanisms for the financial flows—up-front payment, operational funding, milestone payments, royalties, or other kinds of payments.

If these initial conversations go well, then a more detailed discussion of the partnership model and operating principles for the prospective collaboration ensues. Typically, one party proposes a draft **term sheet**—a concise summary of the deal terms—which is then further developed in negotiation. A typical term sheet will include several elements:

- Partnership goals.
- Preliminary outline of the high-level project plan, with expected timelines and major milestones.
- Project budget, funding and payment arrangements.
- Definition of each partner's operational responsibilities.
- Key principles for the project structure, including governance arrangements, scientific advice, and project team.
- How important decisions will be made.
- Provisions for early termination.
- Terms regarding IP ownership and confidentiality.
- Mechanisms for sharing benefits from the eventual outcome, such as royalty payments or revenue sharing.

Some of these elements may appear in a separate informal note outlining mutual expectations instead of the formal term sheet, either because they are difficult to incorporate precisely into the contract without cumbersome legal wording or as a conscious effort to enable flexibility in the governance structure.

Once the parties reach an agreement, the term sheet is converted into a legal contract by the parties' lawyers, a process that usually requires at least one further round of negotiation, to clarify detailed points not clearly specified in the term sheet that surface in the contract drafting process or address differences of opinion about the legal wording for some aspects of the deal.

The partnership model that emerges from this process consists of six specific components that can have a material impact on how the partnership operates later:

- Definition of partnership goals.
- Compatibility of strategic organizational aims.
- Design of payment milestones.
- Principles of the formal project structure.
- Expectations for news flow and publication.
- Provisions for termination scenarios.

Definition of Partnership Goals

The goals of many biopharma R&D partnerships are defined around a specific disease or indication or application. In addition to ensuring a focused, resource-efficient project, such relatively narrow partnership goals may be motivated by a number of other considerations:

- Business development, finance, and legal functions often argue for very specific, tightly defined goals to facilitate the construction of watertight contracts.
- Conventional wisdom in project management favors narrowly defined goals to facilitate unambiguous project monitoring.
- When the partnership is funded on Goliath's side by a specific therapeutic area team, its scope is tied to addressing a specific piece of the therapeutic area strategy.

- David can spread its risk by setting up separate partnerships with different partners to apply the same scientific approach to multiple therapeutic areas; narrow goals allow for this approach by easing the management of IP issues and minimizing conflicts of interest.
- The particular individuals negotiating and setting up the partnerships on both sides often have a preferred application or area of focus in mind.

Nevertheless, as we pointed out in Chapter 2, a biopharma R&D program's most promising application (disease, indication, patient subpopulation) could change significantly over its long duration as new scientific insights emerge and technological advances create new opportunities. More broadly defined partnership goals mitigate execution risk by enabling the project team to maneuver around the challenges presented by scientific findings and operational timelines while taking advantage of opportunities as they emerge. In theory, then, it could make most sense to set loosely defined partnership goals that have a better chance of remaining relevant as the project evolves, especially when it can be difficult to change narrowly defined goals after the partnership begins without getting drawn into another round of long contractual discussions.

As an illustration of the breadth of options for defining partnership goals, consider this example of a collaboration intended to generate drug candidates to treat inflammation. In this case, David is a small biotech with a unique technology platform for modulating inflammation drug targets, while Goliath is a big pharma with a strong commercial franchise in inhaled respiratory drugs, its main product having superior efficacy but an inferior side effect profile compared to its competitors. Here are three alternative options for defining what the partnership aims to deliver:

1. Candidate drugs for asthma or chronic obstructive pulmonary disease (COPD) that exceed a specified set of threshold metrics with respect to efficacy, ADME, formulation, and safety characteristics. Must be at least equal to three primary current offerings in the market with regard to efficacy, ADME, and formulation metrics while exhibiting superior safety metrics.
2. Candidate drugs falling within defined efficacy, ADME, formulation, and safety parameters indicating a competitive and differentiable anti-inflammatory drug for topical application either in the lungs, on the skin, or in the gut.
3. Competitive and differentiable candidate drugs for autoimmune disease applications by any route of administration, plus a secondary goal of identifying biomarkers that might be useful to support personalized medicine claims in such applications.

Option 1 is precise, simple, and easy to monitor, especially if the budget holder for the collaboration is Goliath's respiratory franchise. Option 2 is a better representation of practical realities, since the ADME and formulation characteristics of inhaled, dermatological, and some inflammatory bowel therapies are similar. And option 3 might make sense if the mechanism of action being investigated is **unprecedented**, since the team might find the mechanism more suited to intervention in some forms of arthritis or perhaps systemic lupus.

However, adhering strictly to option 1 runs the risk of missing opportunities for additional indications or diagnostic applications. If option 1 (and to some extent also option 2) is adopted, there needs to be a systematic approach to ensure that the learnings from the project are looked at from the perspective of other potential therapeutic (and even diagnostic) applications. The project structure should include mechanisms that facilitate the assets generated by the project to be considered for repurposing if the primary goals are not achieved. For instance, Bayer HealthCare maintains a Common Mechanism Research team of over 100 dedicated scientists who manage a process to do this.[1]

If option 2 or option 3 is adopted, the onus is on the governance process to dynamically manage the focus of the project team's efforts. This can be accomplished in a variety of ways. For example, the Joint Steering Committee (JSC) or other governance forum might set very specific and narrowly defined short-term objectives that are revised frequently as the project progresses and new information emerges. These intermediate objectives ensure that the Joint Project Team (JPT) has a clear sense of what it is meant to be doing at any given time, allow the JSC to alter course by setting new intermediate objectives as new information emerges, and ensure that the overarching goal is kept in view.

Compatibility of Strategic Organizational Aims

For the partnership to operate effectively, its goals must be embraced by both parties. However, that doesn't mean the underlying strategic aims of the two sides must be the same. Rather, they must merely be complementary. In other words:

- The strategic organizational aims of the two parties must not be incompatible; the achievement of one party's aims will not preclude the other party from reaching its goals.
- Each side recognizes, understands, and respects the aims of the other.

In the inflammation drug example mentioned earlier, Goliath may also be operating in parallel a second partnership with an academic laboratory to identify new inflammation drug targets. The three parties involved in these two partnerships may have different underlying strategic aims; for instance:

- ***Big pharma therapeutic area team***: Defend established respiratory franchise; identify another autoimmune area to enter, if the opportunity presents itself.
- ***Small biotech***: Secure cash flow for inflammation team and build credibility for a major investor fund-raising effort in three years' time.
- ***Academic laboratory***: Publish ground-breaking research on inflammation pathways.

These three sets of strategic organizational aims are not aligned—success in one will not necessarily drive or support success in the other two. But each can be achieved without compromising the others, and both of the partnerships (pharma–academic and pharma–biotech) could deliver outcomes that satisfy all three sets of aims; that is, the two partnerships and three sets of strategic aims are not incompatible.

Design of Payment Milestones

Payment forms and schedules are important both to ensure risk and reward are shared equitably and for how they support the strategic aims of the project. In creating the financial arrangements, and in particular the conditions that trigger milestone payments, careful thought must be given to the behavioral incentives provided by different scenarios. For example, the effect of an excessive back-end loading—the practice of paying as little as possible in the early stages of the collaboration—reduces the financial risk for Goliath, whose negotiation team may think this arrangement incentivizes David to work as efficiently as possible. In practice, however, particularly when David is engaged in several partnerships with different Goliaths, this practice can have the opposite effect. Extreme back-end loading means David needs frequent cash injections to stay afloat, and it will prioritize efforts on those activities with a higher likelihood of near-term cash flow. If a collaborative project is having trouble making scientific headway, David may decide to concentrate its attention and resources on other partnerships yielding more promising results—and more immediate returns. The deprioritized project will then fall even further behind, and pretty soon everyone in David will have given up on it; the partnership will eventually be canceled by Goliath for lack of compelling scientific results.

In another scenario, milestones are very tightly defined in the contract, which simplifies the legal and project monitoring aspects of the project. But the close definitions discourage the project team from looking for other possibilities when the original premise does not pan out exactly as anticipated. Even worse, David, to ensure continued receipt of its milestone payments, could carry on working to generate outputs that satisfy the original milestones even when it does not make scientific sense to do so, pushing the project off the path of optimal value creation. Such a phenomenon is not dissimilar to the historical practice of biopharma companies incentivizing in-house discovery groups based on volume targets for candidate drugs that survived preclinical toxicology testing—the companies often ended up with a lot of placebo compounds.

Thus, as with project goals, it makes sense to define milestones more broadly in the contract and allow the governance process to determine more specific definitions for completion of each stage as the work develops. Even more pragmatically, the contract could allow the JSC to deem that the relevant milestone is contractually achieved if it decides that the project should continue on to its next stage. The formal agreement would, in this scenario, define only the minimum number of major milestones in order to structure the financial arrangements. A more detailed project plan should be developed to help estimate expected timelines, costs, and resource commitments, but these should not be locked in; rather, such plans should be provisional, giving the JPT leeway to detail the actual plan after the deal is signed, and to modify it as evolving scientific and marketplace realities dictate.

Principles of the Formal Project Structure

The key principles guiding the governance and operation of the collaboration need to be agreed on before the deal is consummated. While all the details of a project's development process need not be defined in advance—these will be established in the project set-up phase—it is essential that both parties agree at the outset on the main elements and share expectations for the resources and time needed for governance and operations. Most collaborations include separate structures for governance and operations, with some characteristics of each specified in the partnership agreement.

Collaboration governance will be overseen by the JSC or a similar committee, which will steer the collaboration's direction and have the final say in all the important decisions. It is typical for a project agreement to specify the approximate number of individuals from each party to be included in the JSC, including their primary roles and the expertise that will be represented; specific names need not be decided at this point. Project governance may also include a scientific advisory board (SAB) comprising independent experts who provide guidance around technical and scientific issues. Where an SAB is used, it is typical for the agreement to specify the approximate number of individuals on the board and the expertise required. As with the JSC, no specific names need be decided at this point.

Day-to-day operations will be executed by the JPT. Again, the agreement will usually specify the approximate number of individuals on the JPT and the functions represented. It is normal practice to have JPT membership mirror many of the functional roles—the team will include a person from each party for each key functional area, even when most or all of the activity in that area is carried out by just one party. This arrangement creates clear communication channels and allows the team access to networks in both organizations.

Expectations for News Flow and Publication

David and Goliath will often have very different approaches, and needs, with regard to news flow. For many David organizations, publication of some kind, whether as academic articles or press releases, is essential to survival and often closely linked with their *raison d'être*. Small biotechs, especially those listed on the capital markets, need a constant stream of news to keep their investor base (and potential investors) interested. Even neutral tidbits regarding "something happening" at the company help keep it in the public eye. These companies will be particularly hungry to share news of positive developments as the next funding round approaches. Academic groups, on the other hand, need to publish original findings as a regular stream of scientific papers in highly ranked academic journals to support their grant-seeking efforts. Goliath, on the other hand, may wish to delay or suppress publication in order to maintain a competitive edge.

Thus, mutual expectations for publication and external communication need to be established in advance. Goliath needs to recognize the real news flow needs of its David partners and agree in advance on what types of information can be published or reported, by whom, and when in the collaboration timeline. For example, the design of a sponsored research program between an academic laboratory and a big pharma should incorporate mechanisms allowing publication of some aspects of the work being sponsored, despite the understandable concern of the biopharma sponsor about the release of information that could be useful to competitors. One approach could be a two-component structure for the sponsored work; for example:

- Confidential experiments are conducted at the academic laboratory using unique tools and tissue samples, creating a CRO-like arrangement.
- Research work within a broad scope agreed on with the sponsor is publishable as long as no proprietary secrets

are revealed. This part of the agreement creates a resource for speculative work that can lead to valuable insights and new opportunities for the sponsor while providing support for new research and publication opportunities for the academic researchers.

David, on the other hand, must be realistic about Goliath's needs and flexible about what, when, and where to publish. Sign-off procedures should also be defined, to ensure everyone knows what will be published. Not providing clear guidelines for publication can increase stress and contribute to distrust.

Provisions for Termination Scenarios

A potentially thorny issue in negotiating a collaboration concerns the contractual provisions for terminating it. Both sides want the collaboration to succeed, of course, but the reality is that many projects do not lead to new drugs—many collaborations will fail either to fulfill their initial scientific promise or to achieve market acceptance. Partnership goals that are more broadly defined might allow a project in this situation to find renewed purpose in a different direction, but sometimes, it's not possible to continue. David may not have the resources to support the new direction, or Goliath's portfolio management approach may render the partnership in question unnecessary or irrelevant even if it has been making good scientific progress.

Most partnership contracts specify conditions under which one party can terminate the collaboration, or scenarios under which the collaboration can be terminated jointly. It is important to incorporate hand-back provisions that specify how assets, data, and IP dedicated to or developed by the project will be returned or shared in the event that the collaboration is terminated. IP, in particular, can be a delicate issue in the event of a terminated collaboration, especially if its disposition is not clearly specified in the contract.

In the worst cases, a situation develops in which, in the words of one David CEO, "The project just sits there, neither dead nor properly alive. For internal political or external investor relations reasons, it suits one side to not admit that it no longer makes sense. So it continues to clog up the system, using up some of our capacity and management attention even if it is not being seriously pursued." The project, and the individuals working on it, are left stuck in limbo. One way to protect against such a scenario is to incorporate contractual clauses that deem the partnership to be terminated (hence triggering the hand-back provisions) if the project has not made it to certain stages or achieved certain milestones within a defined time, unless both parties decide that it should remain active.

Due Diligence Misconceptions and Blind Sides

Once both parties have agreed to the formal term sheet, but before the deal is signed, each organization needs to complete a formal **due diligence** process. The object of due diligence is to validate the key assumptions underlying the term sheet and other expectations, assess the risks identified in the negotiation process, and try to uncover any risks that have not been anticipated. The results of due diligence determine next steps—depending on findings, either or both partners could choose to proceed as per the term sheet, negotiate modified terms to compensate for risks that are now better understood, or decline to sign the deal at all. While a detailed exposition of due diligence and how it is conducted is beyond the scope of this book, some common misconceptions and blind slides should be highlighted.

Traditionally, due diligence involves looking closely at the legal, financial, scientific, and commercial aspects of the deal. In parallel, for potential collaborations, Davids will also want to assess the prospective Goliath partner's **external collaborative**

quotient (ECQ)—that is, examine how open the organization is to working collaboratively with outsiders and how well developed is its capacity for doing so.[2] It may not be possible to conduct a formal assessment, but Davids should consider a few pertinent questions, such as:

- How often has Goliath worked with external partners? In what kinds of partnerships? In which direction is the trend moving?
- What do others who have collaborated with the company say about their experience?
- How open have Goliath's people been, especially those in operational roles, when they have interacted with David's in the due diligence process? How did Goliath's people react when David's asked complex or challenging questions?

It's important to make this consideration a conscious part of the due diligence process. Some David organizations, blinded by Goliath's money and track record, fail to dig more deeply into what Goliath can and cannot provide besides funding. In one case I was party to, although Goliath had a strong track record for the indication in question, it lacked the know-how to resolve a challenging CMC issue thrown up by the unusual chemistry of David's compound. Yet both David and Goliath assumed that Goliath's resources could fix the problem. "We've been making drugs a long time, this shouldn't be an issue," one of Goliath's executives said to me. David bought into this thinking and agreed to some rather aggressive timelines in the milestone definitions so as to synchronize the project with an upcoming patent loss on one of Goliath's key products. Only when the project was in process was the gap truly understood. As a result, the project was delayed several years, David got into financial difficulties when the milestone deadlines were missed, and the project ended up many times over-budget.

Similarly, some Goliath organizations can be blinded to potential difficulties by the appeal of an obvious commercial fit. A partnership that promises to yield a product that is a natural fit for the sales force is always tempting, especially if the current product will come off patent in the meantime. But a deal with a good commercial fit but somewhat suspect scientific rationale, or one in which the incremental benefits of the new product do not represent value for money to healthcare payers, will not likely pay off. The corresponding pitfall for David organizations is being blinded by the promise of a big market—a small market your product can conquer is always better than a big one where it is not competitive, and a small market is infinitely better than a product that never reaches the patient because of a mismatch in resources or goals.

Last but not least, two deal valuation pitfalls could afflict either party when quantifying the value of the deal with a financial NPV approach: inaccurately valuing a future application or ignoring the option value of a project. The first is the danger of under- or overvaluing a future application owing to lack of market data. Forecasting high growth rates on existing revenues by projecting historical performance forward is fairly easy; it takes courage and out-of-the-box thinking to argue for significant revenues in unformed markets without track records. It is easy to assign overly low probabilities for revenue streams from new markets and overly high probabilities for well-established markets. Hence, established markets are often overvalued and new markets undervalued in NPV calculations.

The second valuation pitfall is ignoring the option value. The underlying science for almost any project usually has wider application areas beyond those defined in the collaboration agreement, supporting data for which could well emerge in the course of the partnership. A drug that could work for multiple indications or occupy different positions in a disease treatment regimen is always worth more than a single-application product.

It makes sense, then, to bake into the assessment some estimate of the extent to which the initial project focus could be broadened, or alternative applications could be pursued, if the primary focus turns out to be less viable than expected.

Building a Foundation

Rigorously assessing potential partnerships, both for strategic and cultural fit and for the value of the outcomes they promise, is the first step in establishing a successful, productive collaboration. The second important step is to design a partnership model that makes sense for both parties and addresses the key opportunities and risks inherent in the collaboration. Having built these twin foundations, the next two chapters deal with the following steps—creating an appropriate, supportive project structure and navigating the execution stages of the project.

Chapter Notes

[1] See Bayer HealthCare, "Common Mechanism Research: A Second Career for Active Substances," https://healthcare.bayer.com/scripts/pages/en/featured_news.php/40.

[2] *Collaborative quotient* is a concept used by some writers to denote the willingness and capacity of an organization's people to work effectively with each other to solve problems and create new innovations. See, for example, Rajeev Mishra, "Collaborative Quotient Is the Secret to Creating Value at Your Company," *Entrepreneur*, February 20, 2015, http://www.entrepreneur.com/article/243140. With ECQ, we extend this concept to external collaborations.

Chapter 7

Setting Up the Project Structure

Once the deal is signed, the structures and personnel must be put in place to execute the project. While most bilateral collaborations share a very similar project structure, selecting the people who will populate that structure is a critical step, deserving of careful attention. Project team members and project leaders must be open-minded, flexible, and adaptable, as well as technically and scientifically excellent.

In this chapter, we discuss the considerations important in setting up the details of the project structure—how the collaborative project will be organized, conducted, and governed, and—most importantly—by whom. This is a key activity in the transition period between the signing of the deal and the commencement of the project's operations.

Formal Structure

At one level, the formal project structure comprises the various committees and teams set up to govern and operate the project, their mandates and formal decision processes, and the technical and management roles involved. Increasingly, most bilateral partnerships are employing essentially the same formal structure with only minor variations, to the point that most industry insiders would regard it as standard practice. That structure includes components for governance, project operations, and alliance management. The specific terminology and some of the details can vary from one organization or partnership to another, but the underlying structure is largely the same in most biopharma R&D partnerships.

However, the observed effectiveness and efficiency of this structure seems to vary widely across individual partnerships. What makes the difference in my experience is the people involved, their individual attributes and motivations, the expectations they have for how the partnership journey will go, and the mindset they adopt when they engage with each other.

Governance

Overall governance for the collaboration is assigned to the joint steering committee (JSC), which determines the partnership's priorities, allocates the budget, sets the rules for how things get decided and done, interprets the contract in the event that some ambiguity surfaces, and otherwise makes all the important decisions to steer the collaboration. Many JSCs are quite compact; they rarely have more than a dozen members, including nonvoting participants such as the co-leaders of the operational team and the alliance managers. Many projects, particularly joint endeavors and sponsored R&D programs, strive for a high degree of consensus in their JSCs. Indeed, the desire for consensus decision making is increasingly common in value-added supply and IP transfer arrangements, as well, notwithstanding the more obvious buyer-seller nature of these partnership models. Despite the asymmetry in scale between the parties in a David & Goliath collaboration, it is not unusual for each side to have the same number of voting JSC participants.

Consensus may be the ideal, but the reality is that JSC members represent their parent organizations' wishes—which means it may not always be easy to reach consensus. Scenarios not anticipated by the partnership agreement can complicate relations, and strategic decisions made higher up the management chain of the parent organizations can affect the partnership, driving that side's JSC members to push for a particular direction. Hence, maintaining consensus is an active endeavor, one that effective JSC chairpersons see as an important part of their role. Still, parties should recognize that a failure of consensus is possible and create procedures for escalating or arbitrating decisions when no consensus is achievable, unless this eventuality is already anticipated in the contract.

Some partnerships find it helpful to also maintain a scientific advisory board (SAB). Typically, this committee comprises a mixture of experts in the scientific domain of the collaboration, the functional disciplines where the biggest challenges are expected, and the expected application areas. For example, a drug discovery partnership focusing on a particular family of neuroscience drug targets might want an expert in the drug target class known as G-protein coupled receptors (GPCRs), a specialist in a hard-to-interpret *in vivo* model that is essential to the project plan, and a physician key opinion leader (KOL) in neurology. Beware of selecting scientific experts too narrowly. As one academic principal investigator told me about a project:

> Our pharma sponsor insisted on having several eminent practicing rheumatologists on our advisory committee since its primary interest was in arthritis. However, our agreed collabo-

> ration objective was to find new anti-inflammation drug targets. These rheumatology experts struggled to see the wider universe of potential applications, nor could they properly interpret the readouts when we tested our mechanism of action hypotheses in models of other autoimmune conditions.

An alliance comprising several major collaborations between the same two parties might be overseen by a joint alliance steering committee, to which the steering committee for each individual collaboration reports. In this case, some companies use *JSC* to refer to the overall alliance steering committee; individual collaborations are overseen by joint operating committees (JOCs) or joint review committees (JRCs). In another variant of this structure, in this case for a late-stage product development program, an overall steering committee might oversee several operating committees, each responsible for a different facet of the project, such as the clinical program, prelaunch marketing activities, and manufacturing scale-up.

In another possible scenario, a partnership could comprise many small, independent collaborative projects under the umbrella of a single strategic alliance. All of these projects would ultimately report to the same JSC, or sometimes to an intermediate JOC or JRC that oversees operational aspects, leaving only the most important strategic decisions for the JSC.

Project Operations

Project operations are carried out by the joint project team (JPT), which leads the day-to-day activities of the collaboration. The formal partnership agreement (and other documented expectations, if any) defines the main activities of the collaboration, the relative contributions of each party, and the main functional disciplines to be represented in the JPT. Typically, most of the functional areas are mirrored—each function is represented by a person from each side of the partnership, regardless of which party is conducting most of the work in that functional area.

The JPT is usually headed by a pair of project leaders, one from each side, who together are ultimately accountable for the collaboration. In an industry-academic collaboration, the academic leader is usually referred to as the principal investigator and his or her industry counterpart is often called a **project champion**; this terminology reflects the prevalence of sponsored research programs in this space. In a large collaboration, or if the project leaders are working on a number of important external and internal initiatives, project managers will handle the day-to-day coordination of project tasks and logistics, leaving the project leaders to focus on scientific issues.

The relative split of responsibilities between the two project leaders depends to a large extent on the partnership model being deployed. In a value-added supply, IP transfer, or sponsored program model, where the vast majority of the work is conducted by one party, the project leader from the other party mostly plays a consultative and advisory role, although both leaders need to agree on major decisions. Whatever the partnership model, the more interactive the partnership variant, the greater the day-to-day involvement of both project leaders. For instance, in an IP transfer model where the originator is heavily involved in customizing the IP for its partner's use, both project leaders would likely be involved on a daily basis. In joint endeavors, where both sides conduct a significant amount of work, both project leaders are heavily involved.

In a large collaboration, many of the people working on it may not actually be part of the JPT. Rather, subteams conduct specific tasks, each led by or accountable to one of the JPT members, with the mirror member monitoring progress. Some of the subteams will have participants from both organizations, while others will consist of people from only one organization, depending on the team's function and the relative expertise and resources of the two partners. When a subteam includes members from only one partner, the monitoring role of the mirror JPT member is theoretically sufficient to facilitate transfer of relevant expertise and learning from the subteam's work. In practice, the mirror member may not have sufficient time or attention to follow the subteam's work closely enough. In that case, it might make sense to assign another, less senior person (who is likely to have more free time) to follow the work of the subteam. In joint endeavors adopting a co-creative approach, many of the subteams will be joint. Even those joint endeavors taking a divide-and-conquer or pass-the-baton approach often have at least one person from the other party on most subteams to facilitate speedy and effective information exchange.

Alliance Management

Alliance management is concerned with both governance and project operations, and at the same time distinct from them both. Alliance managers operate in the white space between governance and operations, with the sole aim of ensuring that the partnership runs smoothly. Their role is to be watchful and resolve any problems that might arise with respect to the operational and financial arrangements of the partnership. Alliance managers are typically nonvoting members of the JSC and may participate as observers or facilitators in some formal JPT meetings.

Not all partnerships have formal alliance managers, as the function is common as a dedicated role only in the larger Goliaths. In many cases, a partnership will have a formal alliance manager from only one side (usually Goliath), although the other side (typically David) will sometimes nominate an opposite number in response, even if the alliance manager function is only a part-time role for that person.

Alliance managers and their role in making partnerships function smoothly are discussed in detail in Chapter 9.

Selecting JPT Members

Selecting the right personnel to staff a collaborative project may be the single most important factor in the project's potential for success. Biopharma R&D projects are complex, and collaboration adds yet another level of complexity. Effective JPT members approach their work with a particular mindset—one rooted in flexibility, adaptability, and openness to collaboration—and bring technical and functional strengths to the team.

The Right Mindset

The very long road traveled by the typical biopharma R&D program demands a certain mindset, one capable of navigating unexpected problems and pursuing unanticipated opportunities. This is doubly true when working with external partners. The process of staffing up the project structure, whether from internal personnel or through recruitment, needs to bear that journey in mind. Participants for a collaborative project must be selected with three important expectations:

- Participants must recognize that they will be required to negotiate an adaptive journey.
- They must be prepared to work with others in a win-win problem-solving process.
- They must be able and willing to establish trust and build personal relationships with their counterparts in the partner organization.

Given the long, unpredictable course of most biopharma R&D projects, participants in any collaboration must recognize that they will negotiate an adaptive journey in which both problems and opportunities will emerge unexpectedly. Data from one of the experimental studies might suggest a different scientific direction that could lead to a much earlier start of human trials, perhaps in an indication with a much smaller potential market size than the original program promised. Or the cost of conducting a study as initially planned might exceed the available budget. Potential detours and unexpected deliberations of this nature are the norm. In these kinds of circumstances, participants will need to be able to reassess their approach and weigh the pros and cons of the potential paths forward. In fact, adapting the plan as new information emerges and adjusting intermediate goals, budgets, and timelines—in some cases, even negotiating new milestones and partnership goals—will be a key part of their job.

Potential partnership staff will need to recognize that their best chance of innovating the optimum solutions and creating the most valuable opportunities in this adaptive journey is to work with their counterparts in a collaborative, win-win problem-solving process. The aim is not to win a particular battle for a larger slice of the pie, but to grow the pie together with the partner organization, drawing on both the capabilities and insights of the individual participants and the strengths of both organizations. Participants need to be open to a give-and-take relationship and willing to consider the different ways of thinking and working that external collaborators bring.

Finally, participants must work proactively to establish trust and build personal relationships with their working counterparts in the partner organization. This work, which will take time and effort on the part of everyone involved, represents a personal manifestation of the collaboration tax.

The Single-Discipline Perspective: Seeking Technical Excellence

Since most collaborative biopharma projects will focus on a particular therapeutic area or application, experts in the relevant disciplines and technical functions will likely form the core of the JPT. For these discipline representatives, functional competence is the starting point for JPT membership. Most organizations will be tempted to field the most technically or scientifically qualified person available in each of the functional disciplines that will be represented on the JPT. However, I have seen this tactic backfire in partnership situations. The best scientist in a particular field may have very strong opinions about how things should be done, which may not align with those of his or her opposite number from the other side—a clash of egos almost inevitably ensues. Furthermore, deploying the company's most senior expert on one project will limit the time that person can give to other projects. A practical approach that works well is to assign to the JPT a less-experienced scientist who is open to new ways of doing things and well regarded by peers, and arranging for the senior expert to be that person's technical mentor or adviser.

However they are selected, discipline representatives on the JPT should be well networked within their disciplines and across their parent organizations, so that they can draw upon the expertise of the wider organization through their discipline networks. They should also be able to identify the right people for specific subteams and access other scientific experts for advice and input when technical challenges arise.

Discipline representatives must also have an open mindset in engaging with their opposite numbers. They should like learning how other people do things and be open to different ways of thinking, while at the same time being able to ask difficult questions tactfully and willing to challenge the answers to those questions when necessary. In the past, there has been a lot of emphasis on having people able to work across different national cultures, but this is less of a challenge in today's globalized industry than it was; the difference in organizational cultures can be much more of a challenge for some.

Discipline representatives on the JPT must also be comfortable sharing leadership. They will need to consult with their mirror counterparts, keep them updated on progress within the relevant functional area, and make many decisions jointly. This kind of peer-to-peer partnering does not come naturally to many scientific managers. Operating effectively as a co-leader is a skill that improves with practice and experience, although the learning curve can be accelerated by providing an experienced mentor or coach.

The Cross-Disciplinary Perspective

Beyond these single-discipline considerations, some of the problems and opportunities the JPT will face will require integrating multiple disciplines or working across discipline boundaries. These will require cross-disciplinary collaborative problem solving. This capability can be built into the team through two approaches, which can be used together: prioritize candidates with relevant experience and balance team composition to provide diversity of thought.

In this case, "relevant experience" refers not to disciplinary knowledge, but to problem-solving experience and mindsets. Collaborations are created around a wide variety of goals—seeking incremental improvement for an existing solution, addressing a well-defined class of problem that has never been adequately solved, or exploring an entirely new domain where the rules of the game are not yet fully understood, for example. Each requires a different problem-solving mindset. "Me-better" drug discovery within a well-understood mechanism of action is a very different challenge from working on an unprecedented drug target or developing an entirely new treatment approach. Experience in the relevant therapeutic area is not sufficient; the team must include someone experienced in the nature of the challenge. Similarly, some companies will be tempted to keep a winning team together. However deploying a successful team to a new project essentially intact without considering the nature of that earlier project in relation to the one currently in question may backfire.

The problem-solving effectiveness of the JPT can also be enhanced by balancing the team's composition to increase the diversity of thought. Engaging a broad range of project experiences, scientific viewpoints, commercial perspectives, logical reasoning approaches, and working styles increases the team's capacity for innovative solutions and decreases the risk of myopic groupthink. What that mix looks like depends on the goals of the project and the personnel available. One approach would be to assemble a team with experience of a wide variety of different project journeys, including:

- Projects that reached their goals within planned budgets and timelines.
- Projects that experienced a tough patch before recovering to reach a positive conclusion.
- Projects that encountered a scientific dead end and were canceled.
- Projects that made good scientific progress but were canceled for commercial reasons.
- Projects that morphed into different projects with a new scientific angle after the original premise proved unworkable.

Another approach would try to mix different ways of thinking, including:

- Top-down versus bottom-up thinkers.
- Optimists versus pessimists.
- Those who like to speak first versus last in a group.
- Those who prefer consensus versus those who like to play devil's advocate.

Diversity of thought is widely seen as essential to radical innovation, but increasing diversity of thought is helpful in every project. Even those following an apparently well-worn path can be accelerated if the team can imagine smarter ways of doing things along the way, for instance, a faster clinical trial program or a cheaper galenic formulation. Innovation and creative problem solving happen along the entire process of new product discovery and development, not just in the innovativeness of the product itself.

Pragmatic Considerations

All other things being equal, some JPT candidates will be preferred because they have influence with senior stakeholders on the JSC or elsewhere in the organization. There is nothing wrong with this line of thinking *per se* as long as it is not the dominant criteria.

Assembling a team with diverse thinking styles may sound idealistic and impractical, especially in a small organization without many staffing options. Even a large organization can have a lot of active projects and be short of available options. Nevertheless, in my experience, adding or changing even one person on the JPT can change the thinking and dynamics of the team considerably.

A pragmatic approach for selecting JPT members is to first develop a draft roster based on functional competence, discipline network, open mindset, and co-leadership experience or potential. The profile of the team can then be tweaked by changing or adding one or two people to account for the nature of project challenge, create diversity of thought, and acknowledge influence.

Selecting Project Leaders

There has been much written about project leadership in biopharma R&D, and some authors draw distinctions between program leadership and project leadership, and between leadership and management. In my experience, excellent biopharma project leaders share several key characteristics and skills:

- They have broad scientific credibility in the disciplines most relevant to their projects. They may or may not be experts in every one of those disciplines, but they can have sensible conversations with functional leads in the core project team.
- They understand conceptually how their projects add commercial value to the business, and they know what kinds of activities and findings have the most impact (positive or negative) on this value.
- They display a passion for their projects and the benefits they can bring.
- They have a strong organizational network that allows them to access additional resources and expertise for their projects when needed, especially when things don't go according to plan.
- They are adept at working with the governance process; they know how to present their issues to senior executives effectively, recognize the broader political and commercial context within which decisions about their projects are being made, and get the right help assigned to their projects.
- They can manage adaptively, navigating their projects through unexpected twists and turns and inevitable ups and downs. This is important for projects at all stages of the value chain, although the nature of the twists and turns varies. In confirmatory development projects, the goals are very specific (NDA, approval, product launch) and the challenge is to find a different path to the goals when unexpected things happen. When unexpected findings emerge in drug discovery or exploratory clinical development, on the other hand, the leader has to decide whether to adapt the goals to capture a different benefit or

stick with the original goals but find a different way of getting there.

- They are skilled in cross-disciplinary integration. This is also important for projects at all stages of the value chain, but again the nature of the integration varies with the type of project. In later-stage projects, it is about coordinating the work of the functional subteams to ensure that their outputs align and are fed through to anyone who needs them. In earlier-stage projects, interdisciplinary problem solving—getting people from different disciplines to solve problems at discipline boundaries—is required.
- They are effective at process management, able to coordinate others engaged in multiple streams of activity while ensuring the project adheres to its timelines and resource budgets. This is particularly important for large and logistically complex endeavors, such as confirmatory development projects focused on completing the Phase III clinical trial program, assembling the NDA, and preparing for the ensuing product launch. It is also an important skill in smaller and more compact, earlier-stage projects, although in my view, the need for it is somewhat overemphasized compared to the relative importance of other skills.

These attributes apply to all projects, whether internal or collaborative. Thus, a good starting point for selecting a collaboration leader is to identify someone with a strong track record as a leader of in-house projects. Four attributes are particularly important for collaborative projects, and so should be considered when prioritizing candidates for an upcoming collaboration:

- Being able to manage adaptively is a critical requirement in collaborations, which are likely to encounter more unanticipated situations and unknown risks than in-house projects. In large part, this is an organizational expression of the collaboration tax—you cannot know everything about your partner before you start working together, no matter how much effort has been expended in due diligence, and even one you know well from previous experience will have internal events out of your line of sight that affect the collaboration. When these events arise, the project leader must be able to assess the situation, reconfigure activities, and steer the team accordingly.

- The project leader should be particularly strong at cross-disciplinary integration. Guiding the collaboration to success will require facilitating collaborative problem solving with a diverse team and integrating capabilities from both organizations while resolving differences of opinion in a win-win way.
- The project leader must have a strong organizational network and be skilled at influencing people across the organization, not just to access resources and expertise but also to generate interest in the project. These attributes can help ensure that the collaboration's work is well understood and appropriately exploited by the parent organization, and it is also strongly appreciated by the other side in the collaboration, as a David project leader noted to me:

> Our collaboration with [Big Pharma X] went extremely well because my counterpart project leader was well connected in her organization, could reach out to additional scientific expertise across X as and when our project needed it, and ensured a level playing field for our project in X's portfolio review process.

- The project leader needs to work effectively with the collaboration's governance process. For David project leaders who have not previously worked with a large organization, this can be a big learning curve. Goliath pro-

> ject leaders will find that coaching their David counterparts and other David participants about how governance operates in their organization is a major activity, as the fate of the collaboration can be strongly influenced by decisions in Goliath forums that are not visible to David.

Three additional project leader attributes are important specifically in the context of a collaboration. Just like the other JPT members, the project leader must have an open mindset; he or she should be open to learning how other organizations think and do things, while being able to challenge the other party when necessary. Also like the other JPT members, the leader needs to be comfortable sharing leadership. This can be especially challenging for an experienced leader of in-house projects used to calling the shots. As with other collaboration capabilities, this skill improves with practice and the help of experienced mentors. Most importantly, the project leader for a collaboration must role model and coach collaborative working and co-leadership behaviors for the rest of the team.

JSC Membership

The JSC has a different role than the JPT, and so requires a different set of core skills. The primary object is to recruit individuals who have the relevant knowledge and experience to provide good counsel to the JPT and to make strategic choices, including pragmatic compromises where necessary. JSC members should also have the organizational authority to push through decisions that are made. From a functional discipline standpoint, JSC members should blend relevant scientific (including medical if relevant) and commercial (especially therapeutic area franchise) perspectives, supported as necessary by viewpoints from the business development, project management, manufacturing, and financial areas. Diversity of thinking and experience of similar project challenges is also needed in the JSC, as on the JPT.

From David's perspective, a very important JSC member from Goliath, is the *de facto* **executive champion** for the partnership; the champion is also beneficial to Goliath, since he or she ensures the value of the partnership is not lost. The executive champion is an individual who has a strong belief in the value of the partnership for Goliath and advocates for it in Goliath's portfolio management process and other internal forums. This is an important role, since Goliath's organization is usually not transparent as far as David is concerned. The executive champion role is rarely a formal one, but the champion's identity is generally fairly obvious from the individual's actions.

Many partnerships start off with such a champion, often the executive from Goliath who was most influential in shepherding the deal through to signing. The challenge is ensuring there is someone to play this role throughout the partnership's lifetime. Since executives tend to move around in Goliath organizations, this can be a real challenge. As a David CEO said to me:

> Quite often, we find that our original executive champion, usually the one from their side who pushed the deal through, has disappeared from the scene within a year or two, having been moved to another role in their organization. It's not always the case that the champion role is automatically taken on by someone else on the JSC from their side. So we've learnt that we've got to start nurturing prospective champions for the operating phases fairly early on, before the original champion moves to their next role.

In David's case, the JSC representatives often pick themselves, as there do not tend to be too many options in small organizations. Goliath should in theory have more options, although availability is an important constraint. Some JSCs have co-chairs, while others have a single formal chairperson who directs proceedings, seeks to resolve impasses, and if necessary makes the final call on tough decisions. Regardless of which approach is adopted, at least one member of each side must work to proactively consolidate the views of their own people and seek alignment with the other side.

Take Time to Do It Right

The formal structure is established and the various teams and committees are populated during the transition period between the signing of the deal and the scientific work actually starting. It can be tempting, especially for David, to try and finish this set-up activity quickly and get started on the meat of the project as soon as possible. In the case of some Goliath organizations, on the other hand, it might take some time to get all of the pieces together.

In spite of the forces pushing for speed, my advice would be to take your time to get this right. Work through all the details and wait for all the right people to get on board, even if it means a delay of a few months. Getting the right structure populated by the right people at the outset, rather than rushing in early with a less than ideal structure and mix of people, will save time in the long run, and may ultimately save the project.

CHAPTER 8
NAVIGATING PARTNERSHIP EXECUTION

Once the project structure is established and the team assembled, it's easy to feel that the hard work is over. But launching a collaboration on a positive note requires careful attention, and maintaining that positive creative energy is an ongoing task. Project leaders and alliance managers must build cohesiveness and understanding, monitor the mood of the collaboration, and work to create opportunities to celebrate wins and recalibrate expectations as necessary.

Having worked through how to set up the project structure, we now turn our attention to the execution phase of the collaboration. Our discussion begins with a close look at the honeymoon period at the very beginning of a partnership. We then discuss managing through the inevitable stage transitions that occur throughout execution. We conclude by looking at the periodic maintenance actions that are helpful for keeping a partnership running smoothly.

Investing in the Honeymoon Period

Once the deal is signed, the teams are formed, and everyone is on board, there is usually an initial period when the activities are straightforward, the outcomes are predictable, and the inevitable personal frictions have not yet developed. After the hard work of negotiating the deal and structuring the project, it can be tempting to simply sit back and enjoy the tranquility of this honeymoon period, which can last for three to twelve months, depending on the nature of the collaboration. Rather than basking in the serene waters of the new project however, project leaders and alliance managers should use this time to build the foundations for success, taking advantage of the positive feelings and goodwill on both sides to establish strong communication channels and foster trust.

Assuming a sensible business rationale, scientific premise, partnership design and project structure are all in place at the outset, using this honeymoon period well, by enhancing the capacity of everyone involved to collaborate effectively and efficiently, is the most important operational determinant of success. It is essential that the JSC recognizes this opportunity and ensures sufficient time and resources are available to exploit the situation. In my experience, those collaborations that invest up-front in this way tend to perform better, all other things being equal on the scientific and commercial fronts. As the head of a David organization noted:

> We make an extra effort to start every major new collaboration by having face-to-face discussions and site visits every four to six weeks in the first year; we rotate a few different people

> each time so that pretty soon everyone in our team has worked face to face and socialized informally with their people. Yes it takes a chunk out of our travel budget, but the mutual understanding and reservoir of trust that you build this way enables quick and effective problem solving when all the unexpected issues start emerging later on, as they often do.

This essential work is part and parcel of the collaboration tax; it should be regarded as a necessity, not a luxury.

There are some practicalities to address in this initial stage. The first order of business is to finalize the details of the project plan while also getting any unresolved issues from the deal negotiation out on the table. In parallel, the partners also need to establish the ground rules for their day-to-day work. At the same time, through these initial interactions, both sides are getting to understand each other better, building relationships and learning about each other's business processes, working styles, and organizational culture. These lessons are at least as important to the long-term success of the project as the technical and operational details being resolved.

Launching the Honeymoon—The Kickoff Event

One effective mechanism for launching the honeymoon process is a kickoff event attended by all of the participants from both sides. This event brings together everyone from across the project structure to work together for a concentrated period to launch the collaboration. Depending on the scale and complexity of the project, such an event could last anywhere from one and a half to four days, ideally with at least one overnight stay to allow for some social events. Typically, the whole JPT and any assigned alliance managers would attend for the entire duration, with members of the JSC, key individuals from the operational subteams, and external scientific advisers participating for at least part of the agenda.

Prior to the event, the participants are usually assigned preparatory tasks, such as assembling initial drafts of the project plan, developing proposals for the ground rules, documenting case studies of successes or failures in similar projects, setting up team-building sessions, and so on. At the event itself, the agenda typically comprises activities aimed at:

- Finalizing the initial project plan, planning the first tranche of operational work, and agreeing on specific actions to be taken before the next set of formal meetings.
- Sharing relevant lessons learned from similar projects and collaborations.
- Defining operating procedures, **key performance indicators** (KPIs), mutual expectations, and other ground rules.
- Getting to know each other, increasing mutual understanding, and fostering interpersonal relationships.

The kickoff event can be a complex undertaking, requiring thoughtful planning and concerted effort from the project leaders and (if they are assigned) the alliance managers, perhaps with the help of external process facilitators. It represents a significant investment of time and money. Nevertheless, a good kickoff event will get a lot of work done in a short time, socialize the participants into the spirit of the collaboration, and ensure the project is off to a good start. I liken the impact of a well-designed and well-executed kickoff event to be like winding up a spring or charging a battery. It will infuse an enormous amount of energy and collaborative fervor into the partnership, which can power more productive efforts.

Joint Project Planning

One of the primary tasks of the kickoff event should be building a shared project plan. Major milestones and a preliminary outline of the project plan will have already been defined as part of the deal negotiation. These items become the starting point for jointly developing a more detailed project plan that both sides buy into.

It is crucial that this work be done together, to build joint ownership of the plan and avoid tension and blaming when something goes awry. It can be tempting to try to save time at this stage, but these attempts can backfire. One approach I have seen employed is to have each side independently complete the activity plan for its own areas of responsibility and then present the result to the other party as a *fait accompli*. This approach allows the team to focus discussion on the interfaces between the partners' work, but it does not build joint ownership of the whole plan and it does not build mutual understanding of the risks and assumptions driving each party's activities. Instead, each side should produce its own draft plan for the entire project, and then these drafts should be worked together by the whole group, improving each plan and defining the interfaces before finalizing the whole. Working out the entire plan together allows each side to not just understand the factors driving the other's activity plan but also provide the benefit of its own experience. In this way, the group will arrive at a plan both sides can support and build strong foundational relationships.

Furthermore, at some point in the project, new information or unexpected environmental changes will likely trigger the need to alter course in order to meet the collaboration goals. Jointly developing the initial plan at the outset is a useful precursor to a process that might well be repeated several times over the lifetime of the partnership.

One aspect of the joint planning process that is often neglected is resolving hanging issues from the deal negotiation. All issues are rarely fully addressed during the negotiation process; often, the deal teams look for ways around some issues in order to get the deal signed. But these issues don't just go away—the project team must now deal with them. As a simple example, if one party expresses concern about the sample size in a key scientific study conducted earlier by the other party, negotiators may well proceed to a deal without resolving whether the study would be rerun, and if so, by whom and under whose budget. Such issues must be put on the table during the joint planning process, and a path must be mapped to address them.

Partnership Ground Rules

More broadly, kickoff participants should establish ground rules for performance metrics, formal meetings, informal communications, and information exchange. These elements will shape how the partner teams relate to each other and how the project is assessed. Even if the organizations have previously worked together, the nature of this specific collaboration may be different, as may be the individuals involved. Or one or both organizations may have altered their internal business processes or systems since the last collaboration. Thus, although what worked previously may offer a useful starting point, it is always helpful to look at things with fresh eyes.

One of the important items to agree on early in the project is the operational KPIs for the collaboration. KPIs have three related purposes. First, they act as an early warning mechanism if the collaboration is starting to go off track, signaling the need for preemptive action. Second, they demonstrate success and achievement, which is important for the morale of everyone involved. And third, they align with alliance performance metrics that one or both parties might have implemented, indicating the project's ongoing strength and relevance to the company's overall partnering strategy.

Typical KPIs may gauge:

- Operational progress and resource consumption relative to project plan, subdivided as necessary by work package.

- Scientific progress relative to previously determined scientific milestones, subdivided by technical area.
- Impact of key news flow items, including scientific publications and news from competitor projects, regulator pronouncements, or payer reimbursement and pricing decisions. This metric can be summarized using a simple three-category coding system that indicates whether in aggregate the surrounding environmental factors are unchanged (=), more supportive (+), or more hostile (–).

The definition of specific KPIs will be determined by the nature of the collaboration and the needs of the partnering firms and the individual participants.

Another set of items the teams should agree on relate to the convening and conduct of formal meetings. These guidelines should cover a number of facets of the planned program of meetings, including, among others:

- The types of meetings to be convened and their purpose; for instance, JPT regular meetings to monitor progress, JSC review meetings to assess outcomes, SAB meetings to provide scientific advice.
- Core agenda topics and participants for each type of meeting and what constitutes a quorum.
- For each meeting type, the frequency, location, length and format (face-to-face, videoconference, or teleconference).
- General meeting style and participant expectations. For example, some companies aim for all attendees at joint team meetings to review the data beforehand and limit each presenter at the meeting to no more than a few presentation slides, in order to focus on the discussion and resulting decisions.
- The format and procedure for meeting minutes. While it is not necessary to record everything that went on during the meetings, it is helpful, particularly in a collaboration,

to document key issues raised and important decisions made over the course of the partnership, thus creating an audit trail.

Meetings are just one form of communication. Participants should also agree on the nature of any other kinds of communication. This might include:

- The routines for engaging in and documenting informal telephone and e-mail exchanges.
- Whether to have brief e-mail updates between formal meetings and the responsibilities for generating these.
- Whether to have formal written status reports or, as an alternative, short summaries in the form of slides at key junctures, and the responsibilities for generating these.
- Protocols for reviewing and agreeing on public communication, such as press releases or submissions to scientific journals.

Finally, kickoff participants must define the platforms and protocols for data exchange and information technology enablers, such as:

- Information-sharing technology platforms and who will host them.
- Data file formats for the different kinds of information to be shared.
- Security and IP protection considerations.
- Technology platforms for teleconferencing and video-conferencing.

All of these items—from KPIs to meeting structures to information exchange—can involve multiple options with various pros and cons and no one right answer. Rather than deliberating too long, the collaboration team should make initial decisions based on past experience, common sense, or gut feel. Over time, small practical adjustments can be made until, through trial and error, both parties are comfortable.

Building Mutual Understanding

As we've discussed elsewhere, personal relationships can be crucially important to the success of a project, but organizational relationships are equally important. Each organization must understand the other's strategy and broader business processes, especially with regard to timelines for regular tasks. This understanding should extend beyond R&D functions to include any other corporate functions that affect the collaboration's operations, such as regulatory, finance, information technology, legal, and public relations. David and Goliath both may have much to learn. Many David personnel may not appreciate the number of different entities that need to be involved at a Goliath organization to get something like a clinical trial design signed off. Conversely, Goliath people may not realize that an entire department at a David organization may consist of just a single person, with a consequent impact on response time.

This honeymoon phase is the time to go the extra mile to building mutual appreciation of the other side's priorities and organizational dynamics. Such insights will be useful later to help each partner understand the drivers behind the other's questions and actions, and anticipate reactions to its own questions and actions. The honeymoon, while there is little tension or controversy, is also the best time to learn about the other side's preferred communication styles and cultural norms. For example, there can be major differences between organizations in terms of how difficult issues are raised or challenging questions asked.

Of course, the process of building this organizational understanding also provides an opportunity to foster personal rapport between individuals who will be collaborating closely. Much of the work of learning about each other's organizations is best done face-to-face, as people are generally more open, warm, and informal when they are in physical proximity, especially in a semi-social environment such as a business lunch, evening reception, or tour of one party's laboratory facilities. Face-to-face meetings also allow insight to be gleaned from body language and other nonverbal cues. Of course there is an added cost in terms of both time and out-of-pocket expenditure to conduct face-to-face meetings, offsite workshops, and business social events, and this investment might seem high given today's sophisticated voice and video telecommunication tools. But there is simply no substitute for face-to-face relationship building—it is essential for the success of the project.

Managing Through the Project's Transitions

As with any project, a bilateral collaboration will develop through several stages of execution. There are two quite different ways of thinking about execution stages, both of which are important for the project leaders (and alliance managers) to be on top of, namely: technical stages (the different steps of the drug discovery and development process that are within the collaboration's scope) and behavioral stages (changes in the group dynamics and emotional states of the collaboration's participants).

Managing Through the Technical Stages

All biopharma projects, whether collaborative or in-house, go through a similar R&D cycle with defined technical stages. The collaboration's positioning in the overall R&D cycle will determine the technical stages it will navigate. For example, in a small molecule drug discovery, the stages might be:

1. Target validation;
2. Compound screening (sometimes called hit finding);
3. Lead generation (sometimes called hit-to-lead);

4. Lead optimization; and
5. Candidate selection.

As another example, the technical stages in a collaboration to design and conduct a major global clinical trial might be:

1. Study protocol design and feasibility assessment;
2. Regulatory application and approval;
3. Site selection, ethics committee approval, and site training;
4. Patient recruitment;
5. Study monitoring;
6. Data cleaning and management;
7. Statistical analysis; and
8. Medical report writing.

While the technical stages are generally understood as linear, projects often do not follow a linear path. The project journey can be rerouted by new information or environmental changes, which can move the project's goal posts. As a result, the project may have to loop back to a previous stage; this is an unavoidable feature of the industry given the current state of knowledge in the biosciences and the complex regulatory and market environment.

For example, a major safety issue with the chemical structure of the lead series that emerges during the lead optimization stage of a drug discovery project could force the team to restart the hit-finding stage. Or, in a clinical trial, a competitor's drug in the same compound class might be denied reimbursement for first-line treatment, forcing the team to refocus its trial on refractory cases and position its compound for second- or even third-line use. Or, in an earlier-stage collaboration with academia, an altogether new line of scientific inquiry might emerge, triggered by unexpected experimental findings. A new subproject might then be initiated within the same collaboration; that subproject will have to go through all the project stages while the original project either continues or is put on hold.

The progress through the technical stages can affect the project structure, as well. Each technical stage requires different functional discipline skills and thus different team members—and sometimes even a different project leader. There might also need to be a transition to a different governance committee. When these changeovers happen, the collaborative momentum can slow as new team members acclimate to the work and the other participants. It can be a challenge to keep everyone aligned and to maintain the trust, mutual understanding, collaborative spirit, and open mindset established earlier in the project.

Transitions of team members are a particularly acute challenge in a collaboration, especially if the new team members have not been socialized into the collaboration during the honeymoon period. Newcomers may lack understanding of the partner organization's working style and culture, and they may be unfamiliar with the collaboration ground rules. They may even challenge some of the established ground rules, as they have not lived through the process of designing and modifying them. In essence, unsocialized new team members unfamiliar with an existing partner increase the collaboration risk. A number of structural tactics have proven useful in mitigating the impact of these enforced changes. These include deliberately involving later-stage stakeholders earlier than they need to be, to allow them to develop needed understanding and trust relationships; having some members of the old governance committee carry over into the new committee; and maintaining the same alliance manager throughout the collaboration.

Managing Through the Behavioral Stages

The structural tactics mentioned above for maintaining collaborative momentum may not always be practical to implement, and rarely are these tactics alone sufficient to overcome the loss of momentum that can occur. Hence, it is also important to proactively monitor and influence the project participants' behavioral stages in order to maintain collaborative momentum. As behavioral science topics are beyond the scope of this book, we will only make brief mention of two frameworks that I have found helpful in partnership situations; you are encouraged to pursue the references suggested to find out more.

Organizational psychologists look at projects from the perspective of the group dynamics of the project team and how they develop over time. The most famous group development model is the one proposed by Bruce Tuckman in 1965,[1] and subsequently updated by him in collaboration with Mary Ann Jensen in 1977.[2] This model describes five stages of team development:

1) ***Forming***. The group members feel each other out with respect to how they might collaborate.
2) ***Storming***. Individual group members challenge and test each other, eventually finding their place in the status hierarchy.
3) ***Norming***. The group develops an effective way of working together as an integrated team.
4) ***Performing***. The group operates very effectively and delivers on its goals.
5) ***Adjourning (or Mourning)***. The group members get ready to disperse as the project winds down.

When new participants come on board with technical stage transitions, the Forming and Storming stages are repeated, and project leaders and alliance managers must work quickly to get the team back into Norming and Performing. Returning to the high-performance stages will be a challenge if the newcomers have strong personalities or a senior status in their organization. You are encouraged to refer to any of the numerous laymen's expositions of the Tuckman model; many provide good guidance regarding what the project leader can do to manage the team through these stages.[3]

Another useful way of looking at team dynamics is through the lens of the team's fluctuating emotional states over time. A helpful framework for this is the emotional cycle of change, first proposed by Don Kelley and Daryl Conner in 1979.[4] This model describes the sequence of emotional states that, for example, a management team goes through when it seeks to make a transformational change in its business strategy or its organization and processes. In my experience, the Kelley-Conner model is also applicable in R&D projects with difficult scientific problems and challenging business requirements—for example, when the project team is seeking a breakthrough technical innovation or needs to create a fundamentally different therapeutic approach or otherwise do something that has never been done before.

The emotional cycle model describes five emotional states that a project team will experience in a predictable sequence as they work to solve a challenging problem (Figure 8.1):

1) ***Uninformed optimism***. At the start of the cycle, participants are impressed by the quality of the team that has been assembled, motivated by the importance senior management has given to the work they are to do, and confident the team can overcome any problem.
2) ***Informed pessimism***. As team members find out more about the nature of the problem, doubt starts to creep in. The more they understand about it, the more they realize just how difficult the project actually is.
3) ***Hopeful realism***. At some point, after different avenues have been tried, the hints of a way forward begin to emerge. Participants begin to think, "We might just be able to do it."
4) ***Informed optimism***. The team's efforts start to generate what looks like a viable solution. Team members be-

come enthused about the prospect and begin to believe that success is possible: "Yes, we CAN do it!"

5) ***Rewarding completion.*** When the goal is reached, team members feel a combination of satisfaction and relief—and increased confidence that the next challenge can be overcome as well.

Figure 8.1. **Fluctuating Emotional States of a Project Team**

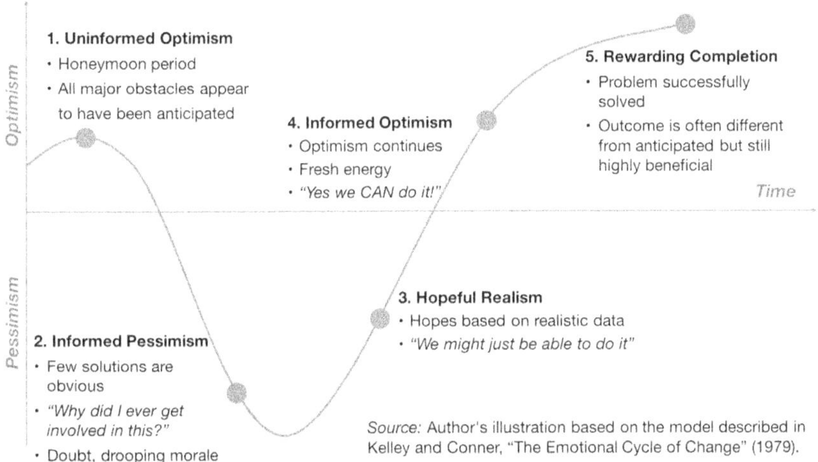

Source: Author's illustration based on the model described in Kelley and Conner, "The Emotional Cycle of Change" (1979).

This model can be applied in both the macro and micro contexts. The macro approach maps the cycle over the entire span of the project; the micro approach treats the collaboration as a series of distinct challenges or problems that need to be overcome, one after the other, each with its own cycle.

At each stage of the emotional cycle, there are a number of helpful actions project leaders can take to support team members and provide encouragement. New participants who arrive with technical stage transitions will be starting at an earlier stage in the emotional cycle, creating challenges for project leaders. At best, these new members can slow the whole collaboration down as they catch up with the rest of the team; at worst, they can drag the others back into their previous emotional states. Hence, it is important that project leaders and alliance managers engage new members appropriately in order to get them aligned with everyone else.

As with the Tuckman-Jensen model, it is beyond the scope of this book to delve into the details of the Kelley-Conner emotional cycle of change, but you are encouraged to follow up the relevant references.[5] Most of what has been written about the emotional cycle of change model relates to its applications in organizational change management situations, but I have also found it useful in the context of an R&D project facing a tough challenge.

Maintaining the Health, Vitality, and Creativity of the Partnership

As a collaboration moves through its stages, the energy level will inevitably fluctuate. The euphoria of the honeymoon period will naturally dissipate as team members get to know each other and settle into the work. This settling is inevitable, but it is important to maintain creative energy and vitality. I have found a number of specific practices to be helpful in fueling collaborative creativity and keeping the partnership energized.

First and foremost, project leaders and alliance managers must maintain the ongoing, open dialogue established in the honeymoon period throughout the life of the project. Any issues that arise need to be brought to the table early and honestly, expectations should be realistic and mutually shared, and impossible promises should not be made. Under the pressure of timelines and stretched resources, there will at times be a strong temptation to skimp on face-to-face or voice-to-voice interactions in favor of electronic written communication—this must be resisted! Interactive contact helps remind everyone why the two sides partnered in the first place and what each brings to the table. These efforts help maintain the all-important collaborative momentum and enhance the team's ability to deal effectively with both problems and opportunities as they arise.

In addition, a number of periodic maintenance activities, consciously pursued, can help sustain a fresh and vibrant atmosphere in the partnership. As the collaboration progresses into its second or third year and beyond, there is a risk of staleness or fatigue emerging, which in some cases can even lead to the development of an antagonistic, us-versus-them climate. As the CEO of a focused biopharma with a large portfolio of collaborations described it to me, "If you're not careful, after a few years you end up focusing on each other's bad points, remembering only those arguments you've lost and completely forgetting why you got together in the first place."

A periodic collaboration **health check** can help avert or alleviate this situation, especially in a long, complex partnership or an alliance involving multiple collaborations between the same two parties. In a health check, which should be carried out at regular intervals, everyone involved in the project is surveyed regarding how their view of the collaboration in terms of its progress on the content, the effectiveness of its processes, and the collaborative working environment. These surveys yield a regular temperature reading that allows leaders to monitor the health of the collaboration and act proactively if corrective action is needed. The formal, detailed survey can be supplemented by informal, broader-ranging one-on-one discussions with selected individuals, conducted by the alliance managers or members of the governance committee. In some situations, it might also make sense to have an independent third party interview a selection of participants at all levels of the collaboration, to gather additional data or assess the need for action.

In the health check process, it is important to engage participants from both sides of the partnership at the same time with the same set of questions. The questionnaire should be developed jointly, with leaders from both organizations, using terminology that is relevant for that specific collaboration or alliance. Leaders should resist the temptation to replicate an off-the-shelf template or reuse a survey from an earlier partnership. An experienced alliance manager related a story to me that illustrates this point:

> Each side turned up with its own standard health check template that they had developed from their last big collaboration, and when we compared them, we realized they used different words for essentially the same things and also contained some common words that actually meant different things! And also, this collaboration was somewhat different in nature to what each of us had done in the past. So we ended designing a new questionnaire, which in the process of doing so, also greatly enhanced mutual understanding of each other's culture and organizational values.

Another means of keeping the collaboration fresh and healthy is the occasional introduction of new faces. New team members may be required by a change in the project's technical stage that requires new expertise, but swapping personnel can also be a good tactic to change the group's perspective on where the collaboration needs to go or to alter the group dynamics. This approach should be pursued with caution, though; new team members can play havoc with group dynamics and the team's emotional cycle, so changes in the team should be made only as part of a carefully thought-through process.

Periodic collaboration team events can also help keep the energy level up and encourage the team. Joint celebrations, to mark significant milestones or important steps forward in the scientific work, with attendant organization-wide recognition of contributors, can revitalize a team. Even smaller moments can be celebrated in some way. Project and organization leaders should never underestimate the motivational benefit of frequent positive recognition of even minor wins.

The astute use of regular collaboration team events, sometimes called retreats, off-sites, or away days, can provide a much-needed opportunity to take stock, realign the team, and reenergize everyone involved. These events are similar to the kickoff event in a number of ways—they sequester the whole team at an offsite location for one or several days to review progress, resolve ongoing issues, make decisions, reaffirm mutual expectations, chart a new direction if one is needed, and otherwise do a lot of work in a compressed, distraction-free time slot. These events can also be good opportunities to introduce new members to the team, say farewell to departing team members, conduct both scientific and collaboration training, and celebrate wins.

Collaboration team events can be held annually at the same time each year; this approach works well for alliances with lots of small, mostly independent projects—each such collaboration will be at a different point in its life cycle but too small to conduct an event of its own. For a larger, more complex collaboration with a long duration, it makes more sense to schedule events at specific points in the project life cycle. In the same way that a kickoff event launches a project on a positive note, well-designed and well-executed collaboration team events will reenergize the collaboration, recharging the team's batteries to attack their challenges anew.

Chapter Notes

[1] B. W. Tuckman, "Developmental Sequence in Small Groups," *Psychological Bulletin* 63 (1965): 384–399.

[2] B. W. Tuckman and M. A. C. Jensen, "Stages of Small Group Development Revisited," *Group and Organizational Studies* 2 (1977): 419–427.

[3] For a straightforward layman's exposition, see, for example, G. Abudi, "The Five Stages of Project Team Development," *The Project Management Hut*, May 8, 2010, http://www.pmhut.com/the-five-stages-of-project-team-development.

[4] First documented in D. Kelley and D. Conner, "The Emotional Cycle of Change," in *The 1979 Annual Handbook for Group Facilitators*, ed. J. Jones and J. Pfeiffer (San Diego, CA: University Associates, 1979). This book is now out of print; a more readily accessible source for explaining the model is David Deviney, "The Kelley-Conner Emotional Cycle of Change," blog post, *I/O Psychology*, November 4, 2010, http://www.executivepsychology.com/workpsychology/2010/04/the-kelley-conner-emotional-cycle-of-change/.

[5] To get started, see the Deviney (2010) article referenced in note 4 and Daryl Conner, "Change Is Easy When People Like It, Right?," blog post, *Daryl Conner*, April 24, 2012, http://www.connerpartners.com/frameworks-and-processes/change-is-easy-when-people-like-it-right.

CHAPTER 9
LEVERAGING ALLIANCE MANAGERS

As big pharmas increasingly externalize their R&D efforts, they look for better ways to ensure results from their collaborations. Alliance managers are an increasingly common part of that effort. Because they can focus on the organizational and people factors at work in the collaboration, alliance managers can help create synergy in ways that leaders concerned with governance or operations cannot. Although alliance managers first appeared in big pharmas, smaller companies that rely on partnerships are also increasingly deploying them to support their collaborative efforts.

In this chapter, we first define what an alliance manager is, then delve deeper into the work of alliance managers, highlighting the regular processes they look after and the tools they deploy and describing some of the problematic situations they are called upon to resolve. We conclude by discussing what makes a good alliance manager. In this discussion, we focus on individual alliance managers. Corporate alliance management groups are discussed in Chapter 10.

What is an Alliance Manager?

When we refer to alliance managers, we mean the people who are responsible for alliance management activities in a partnership. These are the activities conducted to ensure that collaborations proceed to their goals efficiently, effectively, and harmoniously and in a timely fashion. The *raison d'être* of alliance managers is to create synergy from the differences between the two parties, thus enabling the collaboration to deliver on its goals. Everyone involved in the partnership has a part to play in making this happen, but alliance managers lead these efforts. Especially in a David & Goliath collaboration, the differences between the partners can be very stark, and the challenges in communication and cooperation frequent—the task of alliance management is not an easy one!

Alliance managers do not need to be formally designated as such, nor do they need to be engaged exclusively in alliance management full time. The crucial thing is not who the alliance manager is, specifically, but that at least one person from each party has been clearly designated to play this role. In fact, the role can be filled by more than one person; some David organizations do not have any dedicated alliance managers, but delegate the role for each partnership, usually sharing it between the project leader and a member of the governance committee.

What Alliance Managers Do

While the specifics and priorities differ from one company to another, and from one partnership to another, the roles and responsibilities of an alliance manager usually cover seven areas:

1) ***Contract management***. Managing contractual obligations, such as milestone payments; advising collaboration participants on how the partnership contract should be implemented; and if necessary, negotiating with the partner regarding the interpretation of the contract in the event of a difference of opinion between the two sides.
2) ***Progress monitoring***. Tracking progress, including coordinating the definition and reporting of the KPIs as well as leading periodic health checks.
3) ***Process management***. Establishing and ensuring smooth operation of the collaboration ground rules, such as the protocol for formal governance meetings and procedures for decision making, project team meetings, data exchange, and other kinds of interactions.
4) ***Brand management***. Managing how the company as a whole is perceived by the partner, and how the partnership is perceived by people in one's own company.
5) ***Alignment and relationship building***. Leading efforts to increase alignment, mutual understanding, and trust between collaboration participants, including activities such as the kickoff event and periodic collaboration team events.
6) ***Strategic value and risk management***. Identifying the important value drivers and key risks, ensuring those involved do not lose focus on strategic aspects, and leading efforts to mitigate risks and accelerate value creation; looking for win-win opportunities to extend

the relationship by expanding the existing partnership or creating additional spin-off collaborations.

7) ***Change management***. Anticipating changes in project stages or collaboration participants, managing these transitions smoothly, and serving as the partnership's memory, as well as facilitating complex discussions with the partner to map a way forward when unanticipated situations or corporate decisions in either party trigger the need for change.

An important aspect of an alliance manager's working day, some would say the most important, is engaging with people. The key, as many alliance managers have told me, is to know the individuals involved in the collaboration and understand what drives them. Although it may seem counterintuitive, the majority of this communication is internally facing; empirical estimates from the alliance managers I have talked to range from at least 50% to as much as 80% of their work being within their own organizations. The higher end of the range is particularly likely when the organization is new to working with external parties. Sensitizing one's own organization to the partner's differences, explaining how the collaboration operates differently from an in-house project, and selling the benefits of the collaboration internally are critical components of the alliance manager's mission.

At first sight, there might seem to be significant overlaps between what alliance managers and project leaders do on the one hand, and between what alliance managers and business development managers do on the other hand. However, the underlying missions of each function are different. Project leaders drive day-to-day operations to achieve the project's goals in the best possible way. Business development managers find, structure, and complete deals that are in the best possible interests of their own organizations. Alliance managers focus on the collaborative process and the people involved; their function is to ensure that communication and decision-making processes maximize the partnership's potential strategic value and manage its inherent risks. Alliance managers should ideally work closely with their business development counterparts to design the partnership model as it is being negotiated, so that communication pathways are built in from the outset. They work closely with project leaders over the course of the partnership.

Alliance managers also operate in the white space, taking on issues that no one owns, especially with regard to topics that would not even arise in an in-house project. Although some part of their daily work involves overseeing recurring processes and routine tasks, such as health checks, they really add the most value as troubleshooters, addressing complex or difficult situations, as one experienced alliance manager intimated to me: "If it goes well, it's no thanks to the alliance manager, but if it does not, then we are the ones who are supposed to fix it!" A key attribute of alliance managers—and a prerequisite for building strong relationships—is a high level of comfort with give and take. As one experienced alliance manager noted: "Sometimes you need to give concessions, to be perceived by your partner that you respond positively to their needs. This does not mean you should say yes every time. You just can't say no all the time."

Battling Misconceptions

Goliath companies largely recognize the value of alliance managers and embrace them. All the Goliath alliance managers I have come across were generally positive and enthusiastic about their role in helping collaborations succeed. David organizations, however, have been slower to adopt the alliance manager model, and there are still some in these organizations who do not recognize its value. Rather, they view their partners' alliance managers as policemen, primarily focused on managing contractual obligations and monitoring progress. I encountered several instances of such sentiments in my research; for example:

> You need scientists interacting with each other if you want to get somewhere. You don't want the alliance managers coming in between the two. To be honest, I'm not sure what their alliance manager adds that can't be done by a good project leader on their side.

> My interactions with big company alliance managers have been much the same—pretty hopeless! They're usually corporate bean counters who jump in and don't really understand what's going on.

Given these attitudes, Goliath alliance managers sometimes must prove their worth at the outset of a collaboration. Especially with David organizations that are comparatively new to partnerships, or that have had negative experiences with other alliance managers, a charm offensive is sometimes needed to defuse suspicion.

To be fair, David's overall perception of Goliath alliance managers has improved in recent years. In my interviews, a number of appreciative David managers and scientists enthusiastically endorsed the alliance managers they've worked with; to illustrate:

> Their alliance manager is great. He predicts what's going to come, helps avoid problems; he's really impressive, by far the best I've seen.

> Their alliance managers were definitely different from others we've worked with. They went out of their way to get to know our people and understand how to engage with us informally. They also saw their role as socializing our project internally in their organization to make sure that when the asset is transitioned fully to their company, it would be viewed as an internal one.

This positive trend should continue as some Goliath organizations begin seeing alliance management as a training ground for their most talented people, a practice one Goliath executive described to me:

> The development path for top talent and potential senior management should include experience as an alliance manager. Partnerships are now an integral part of our business.

Conversely, some David personnel, including unfortunately a few in leadership positions, feel that their own alliance managers should concentrate on negotiating milestone payments, increasing the alliance budget, and creating additional projects. These are part of the alliance managers' work, but only a part; pushing them to focus only on these aspects limits the value they add and, perhaps worse, could create tension with the Goliath partner.

Alliance Managers at Work: Collaboration Processes and Tools

Effective alliance managers are engaged in every phase of a project, from the negotiation onward. In the early stages of designing the partnership model, involving the alliance manager can help mitigate the handoff problems that sometimes plague the transition from the deal team to the execution team. During due diligence, an alliance manager with a breadth of experience in previous partnerships can help assess the prospective partner's external collaborative quotient (ECQ) and evaluate its operational and cultural fit. At the very minimum, the alliance manager should follow the negotiation process to understand the rationale for particular elements in the partnership agreement—as well as what is not in the agreement, the unwritten assumptions and implicit compromises made to achieve an acceptable deal. This understanding of the spirit of the collaboration will be essential when the alliance manager is called upon to negotiate a workable interpretation of the contract after the collaboration is in full swing.

As the project begins operations, alliance managers are most visible in the alliance management processes required for all partnerships. They will typically be involved in:

- Organizing and managing the launch, including the kickoff event.
- Defining and later adapting the project plan.
- Establishing operational ground rules for governance and project meetings, defining KPIs, and creating processes for decision making, information exchange, and other forms of communication and interaction.
- Identifying and creating consensus around the important value drivers and key risks for the collaboration, and re-visiting these key elements periodically as the collaboration develops.
- Initiating and overseeing periodic maintenance activities such as collaboration health checks, team events, and milestone celebrations.
- Onboarding new project team and governance committee members as the collaboration moves through the different stages of its technical life cycle.
- Coordinating the closure of the collaboration when the time comes.
- Capturing lessons learned for future collaborations.

These collaboration processes are set up and driven jointly by the alliance managers and the project leaders. Alliance managers focus on the process aspects of the project, freeing project leaders to give their full attention to the content aspects, although the precise split in responsibilities will depend on both organizations' norms. For example, in the initial project plan, project leaders are typically responsible for the content of the plan and alliance managers typically focus on how team members work together to create it, who is involved from each side, and how best to get buy-in and approval from the governance committee. In a similar vein, when capturing lessons learned, project leaders concentrate on scientific and project management insights while alliance managers concentrate on the learning regarding collaborative working processes and approaches.

Alliance managers will also be engaged in the design and implementation of appropriate information technology arrangements to connect the two organizations. This is a natural outgrowth of their role, as these arrangements are critical to support the collaboration processes that are the focus of the alliance manager's work. The technology interface is an important element to get right from the outset of a collaboration; care needs to be taken to ensure that the systems, and how people interact with them, do not get in the way of relationship building and an open interactive dialogue. This is a delicate balance. I have on several occasions seen systems that are meant to support collaboration have the opposite effect, in part because they are too efficient, reducing the need for collaborators to engage in real-time conversations.

In supporting collaboration and monitoring the project's health, alliance managers may make use of a wide variety of tools and approaches. These may include:

- Key documents.
- Flow diagrams and checklists for collaboration processes.
- Meeting agendas and meeting management checklists.
- Kickoff and team event designs.
- Matrix diagrams and other analytical charts.
- Questionnaires to assess group dynamics.
- Health check surveys and interview guides.
- KPI definitions and dashboard reporting formats.
- Team-building exercises.

A technology-enabled sharing platform can make this toolbox available to the entire community of alliance managers across an organization to implement in future collaborations. But managers must beware of a one-size-fits-all approach. The repository of tools should serve only as a baseline; templates and outlines must be customized and adapted for each partnership. Processes and tools will vary depending on the partner organization's norms, and in any case there are no universal tools or process definitions that are optimal in every situation. The overriding characteristics of the successful alliance manager are a level of comfort with give and take, flexibility, and pragmatic common sense.

Alliance Managers at Work: Problematic Situations

As the key problem-solving interface between their own organization and the partner's, alliance managers are often on the front lines when a partnership starts to get complicated.

In this section, we will adopt the David perspective and walk through a number of challenging situations that can arise over the course of a David & Goliath partnership's life cycle, that you as David's alliance manager will be expected to navigate, such as:

- Corporate changes and portfolio adjustments by the partner.
- Unexpected scientific results and environmental changes.
- Unanticipated resource constraints and budget issues.
- Milestone issues.
- Orphan project syndrome.

Corporate Changes and Portfolio Adjustments by the Partner

As your R&D project moves through its often extended life cycle, many elements of its context will change, including the structures and processes of your partner. Sometimes, those changes are radical enough to threaten the project or force it to change course. Goliath might merge with or be acquired by another company. Or a new Goliath CEO might launch an organizational restructuring process or initiate a strategic review that shifts the company's priorities. At this point, you and your David colleagues need to sit tight and be patient. Your Goliath counterparts will be understandably nervous about what this development means for their careers as well as for the partnership, even before any decisions have been made. You should not be surprised if they start to move a bit slower. It will take some months for any strategic decisions to be made about your partnership, and it is unrealistic to seek any firm commitments from the other side while things shake themselves out. The important thing at this point is to make sure the team keeps going and continues to work as best as it can under the circumstances.

Once Goliath makes its strategic decisions, there are two scenarios. If the partnership continues, then the alliance managers and project leaders face the challenge of getting the collaboration running at full throttle again. In many cases, at least some Goliath people on the project team and governance committee will change. A critical element for the health of the project is whether Goliath's project leader, alliance manager, or executive champion on the governance committee will remain involved. The loss of one or more of these individuals will make restarting the partnership that much tougher, as will the loss of a great number of Goliath team members. Such wholesale change will undo much relationship building and risk undermining the shared understanding that has been developed. At the very minimum, you will need to work with your Goliath counterpart to on-board all the new faces, getting them up to speed on the technical aspects and facilitating relationship building. And you will need to help them navigate the group dynamics and move through the emotional cycle stages quickly. You may well find it necessary to run an offsite collaboration team event to integrate new team members and relaunch the partnership.

On the other hand, Goliath may choose to terminate or scale down the partnership as its portfolio priorities change. This decision may be the result of a portfolio review or strategic reorganization that shifts the organization's focus. Or it may be a consequence of a merger or acquisition—the acquiring company may have a similar project that is further down the track. Or the company may decide to exit the therapeutic area entirely. A termination outcome need not be the result of a radical organizational change; it could occur anyway as Goliath shuffles resources in the wake of its annual portfolio review process.

Whatever the reason for the decision, the first point to bear in mind is that a partnership terminated for portfolio reasons is not a failure on either company's part. With the chances of success in biopharma R&D so low, all Goliath organizations systematically invest in more projects than they can afford to fund all the way to product launch, on the assumption that some will fail scientifically or be deprioritized along the way. A terminated project is just business as usual.

When an enforced termination happens, the onus will be on you, as David's alliance manager, to facilitate a smooth and prompt exit from the collaboration. You will need to focus on getting back the assets, data, and documentation due under the hand-back provisions of the partnership agreement; ensuring that all outstanding financial and other commitments are met; and capturing lessons learned as well as any potentially useful scientific insights before the collaboration team disperses. And you must do all of this while maintaining a professional demeanor and inspiring a positive outlook in disappointed team members. This moment is a true test of an alliance manager's professionalism and diplomacy.

Unexpected Scientific Results and Environmental Changes

As happens in many other biopharma R&D projects, there could come a point in your collaboration when unexpected scientific results or changes in the market or regulatory environment trigger a reconsideration of the underlying project rationale. For example, results from the experimental work argue against the original hypothesis for treating colon cancer on which the collaboration is predicated. A newly published academic paper suggests that your treatment hypothesis might actually be better suited for other forms of cancer. Or the regulatory authority, concerned about recent adverse events in the patient population, announces that it will require more onerous clinical and safety testing, threatening the viability of your project plan. Whatever the reason, the project team needs to revisit the key scientific hypotheses and critical business assumptions underlying the collaboration. In theory, this situation is the responsibility of the project leaders. But you as the alliance manager can play an important role in supporting, guiding, and coaching the leaders to a clear, coherent decision.

The first order of business is to validate the relevance and potential magnitude of the concern or opportunity. For example, if the scientific results are not encouraging, the reasons for those results need to be examined. The experimental protocols and equipment need to be reviewed and different experimental designs may be developed to see if the results can be reproduced. In the case of the regulatory pronouncements, it could make sense, with the help of other resources in Goliath, to engage the regulator in a discussion to clarify their intentions and to seek advice from relevant regulatory and clinical experts.

Whatever the specific situation, you need to work closely with your Goliath counterpart and the project leaders to keep everyone on the project team calm and thinking sensibly. It is important not to react emotionally or jump to rash conclusions. You and your Goliath counterpart also need to engage your governance committee members sensitively, both to buy time for the project team to figure out what the situation really means, and to get help from the wider organizations.

Once the situation is sufficiently understood, a creative mindset is required to develop a path forward. You and the Goliath alliance manager might need to facilitate a change in the partnership goals, or work with your organizational networks to scale down or expand the collaboration's scope, resourcing levels, and timelines. You may even need to amend the partnership agreement or negotiate a different interpretation of it. Here again, diplomacy and a wide network are required, as well as cheerful professionalism. Above all, the alliance manager in this situation must be a calm voice.

Unanticipated Resource Constraints and Budget Issues

Resource constraints and budget issues can arise from a number of sources. It is not uncommon for a collaboration's budget to be underestimated at the time the deal is signed. Changes in the business environment can affect Goliath's overall capacity and impinge on the collaboration. Or David becomes overstretched, either having made too many commitments across its portfolio of projects or having struggled in its most recent fund-raising round. Whatever the reasons, despite an unchanged scientific and commercial outlook, your collaboration now has to make do with less funding and fewer resources than it needs.

Here again, this in theory is a problem for the project leaders; it is no different than the kind of resource questions an in-house project would have to face. If anything, the joint experience and expertise of the two parties ought to result in a smarter solution. However, in practice, this kind of problem in a partnership can trigger the kind of us versus them thinking that puts a heavy strain on the relationship between the two parties. The situation can rapidly spiral out of control into a full-blown contractual dispute. The alliance managers on both sides need to watch for this kind of situation and try to head it off in advance by engaging project leaders in a productive dialogue.

The pragmatic solution usually comes from adopting a similar mindset to that taken by an in-house project facing the same challenges—concentrate on the scientific work that provides the biggest bang for the buck and delay activities not on the critical path. If the constraint is on human resources or equipment capacity rather than on money, then another option to fill the gap is the use of third-party providers. Or perhaps some of the resource-constrained party's responsibilities could be temporarily reallocated to the other party in return for a fair adjustment in the financial terms.

More often than not, the resource crunch is temporary and what eventually transpires is a slowdown in the short term that is made up later, when resources become available again. Given that reality, the real imperative is to avoid damaging the relationship with rash actions or accusations. As the David alliance manager, you need to work with your Goliath counterpart to facilitate a sensible temporary solution that supports the health of the collaboration.

Milestone Issues

Although project milestones may appear to be clearly defined in the partnership agreement, any number of issues can emerge over the course of a partnership. The collaboration can evolve so much that the milestone definitions in the partnership agreement no longer make sense. Or you and your David colleagues may believe that a milestone has been achieved while your Goliath partner does not. Or it may suit Goliath's finance function to delay recording the achievement until the next financial reporting period. Or, conversely, you and your David colleagues may be under pressure from your senior management to get a milestone payment approved as soon as possible in order to get it recorded in the current financial year, even if the work is in truth only 95% done.

Other perverse situations could also arise. You and your David colleagues might be under pressure from your senior management to continue the project work to secure future milestone payments even though it is becoming apparent that the collaboration goals will never be achieved. Yes, this is within the company's contractual rights, but it is neither ethical nor smart from the perspective of maintaining a good partnering reputation. Conversely, Goliath, having lost interest in the collaboration's business rationale, could seek excuses to not make the milestone payments, regardless of the actual state of the project work. These situations are not that common, in fact—what is much more common is one party believing that the other party is trying to do something of this nature!

Renegotiating milestones or agreeing on their achievement and consequent payments is in the sweet spot of the alliance manager's mandate. However, achieving agreement will usually require much more discussion, negotiation, give and take, and sheer common sense than an inexperienced alliance manager realizes. Achieving the mission requires the management of egos, political considerations, and emotional reactions. The contractual definition of milestones is a merely a starting point; both alliance managers and the governance committee chairperson need to recognize that they must anticipate and manage milestone issues. Letting emerging differences of opinion on milestones escalate into distrust and full-blown contractual disputes does not help anyone.

Orphan Project Syndrome

In an ideal world, even if your collaboration is not a top priority for both parties, it should at least be viewed as equally important by both participating organizations. Unfortunately, however, it is not uncommon for a partnership to lose visibility and management support in one or both organizations, thus becoming orphaned. Orphaning may result from any number of factors, including organizational and environmental changes. Goliath's interest could wither or disappear entirely if your collaboration's executive champion moves to another role or leaves the company. If David has recently raised a lot of funding from the capital markets for its own proprietary projects, its management team may become disinterested in technology licensing partnerships. Whatever the reasons, once it is orphaned, your collaboration will struggle to get the resources, support, and management attention it needs to deliver on its goals.

There are several tactics you can adopt to prevent or at least reduce the likelihood of your collaboration becoming an orphan. One of these is to ensure that the collaboration always has at least one executive champion on each side at all times. This can be difficult, however, because the executives who make the most influential advocates in Goliath are also likely to be dynamic leaders who will make frequent career moves, both within and beyond the organization. So as the alliance manager, you need to be continually on the lookout for prospective executive champions, even when the current champion is actively involved.

Another tactic that can be adopted is to seek Goliath project leaders, alliance managers, or other project members who have strong networks in their organization and who have both the ability and the enthusiasm to sell the collaboration internally. With a little encouragement, these individuals will engage people from across their organization who might find the scientific work or commercial implications of the collaboration interesting.

A third tactic to avoid orphaning is to encourage the collaboration team as a whole to publicize its progress and findings within their own organizations, through poster fairs, a partnership intranet site, or e-mail updates to those across the organization who find the collaboration's activities relevant to their own work. Facilitating frequent but relevant communication at all levels is a key part of the alliance manager's role; it is also your best prophylactic to ensure that your collaboration creates and maintains sufficient mindshare in both organizations. This is certainly a case of prevention being much more viable than cure—once your collaboration has fallen off the radar screen, it can be extraordinarily difficult to attract renewed attention.

Foundations for Resolving Problematic Situations

A strong relationship based on trust and mutual respect is the cornerstone for resolving problematic situations in a partnership. As an alliance manager, one of your primary responsibilities is establishing and strengthening deep, broad relationships between the two parties in a collaboration—between the two alliance managers, the two project leaders, the governance committee members, and other key participants. That work begins in the honeymoon period, continues throughout the collaboration life cycle, and never stops.

Part and parcel of both relationship building and problem solving is honest but sensitively executed communication to:

- Clarify what each side really wants and can actually do.
- Align mutual expectations with regard to each other's roles and responsibilities.
- Anticipate issues and deal with them before they get out of hand.
- Find common ground and pragmatic win-win solutions.

With each issue resolved, the partnership becomes stronger. You know you have a strong relationship when the project demonstrates resilience, responding to changes effectively and efficiently and weathering difficult issues.

What Makes a Good Alliance Manager?

Alliance managers confront a wide range of issues and must work tactfully with people at all levels of the organization to develop practical solutions that are acceptable to both sides of the partnership. This is delicate, consuming work that requires a number of well-developed skills.

First and foremost, good alliance managers have outstanding communication and facilitative leadership skills (or influencing skills) that they exercise with sound judgment and a clear understanding of both parties' business goals and cultures. They are strong advocates for their partnerships in both the partners' and their own organizations. This function is facilitated by the fact that they are natural networkers, well connected with different parts of the organization. A David project leader described his successful alliance manager in this way:

> Our alliance manager built contacts across their organization and spends time finding out what's going on behind the scenes. She is a very warm person whom you could easily talk to, but at the same time is very perceptive of how things are moving, and is not afraid to step in and influence on both sides when the situation calls for it.

Alliance managers must also have credibility to engage with collaboration team members and other personnel across the operational side of the project. That credibility ideally should be based on operational experience in at least some of the functional disciplines that are predominant in the types of projects they oversee.

As the issues they get involved in may be quite complex and multilayered, good alliance managers need to be able to cope with the details of, for example, the contract without losing sight of the big picture. They are usually open-minded and curious individuals, receptive to new ways of thinking, and have probably worked in a number of different roles. And they can focus on what matters most, never forgetting that their role is about optimizing the strategic value of the partnership rather than just managing the contractual obligations.

Since some of the issues they tackle can have difficult political and emotional overtones, good alliance managers also need courage and do not shy away from conflict. "It's not about appeasement," as one experienced alliance manager told me. They often have to do things that are in no one else's area of responsibility, so they need to be self-starters who can anticipate issues and figure out by themselves how to act.

Selection, Training, and Development of Alliance Managers

Intuitively, you might think that the best candidates for alliance manager roles come from the project management or business development ranks. But good alliance managers seem to come from all sorts of backgrounds. They need to have sufficient scientific competencies to grasp at a macro level the key technical issues for the kind of projects they work with, but they do not need to be subject matter experts in any specific technical discipline. The important thing is that they possess the underlying personal attributes and skills required.

Experienced alliance managers, as well as those project leaders and scientists who have worked closely in several collaborations with good alliance managers, often have an innate sense of who might make a good alliance manager. Thus, a productive starting point when seeking to recruit more alliance managers is the networks of these people.

Training is important for new alliance managers, especially in skills that are not usually taught, such as conflict resolution, and to familiarize them with the repository of process definitions and supporting tools. In some biopharma companies, the professional certification of their in-house alliance managers through the pan-industry Association of Strategic Alliance Professionals (ASAP) is seen as a way to professionalize the role. Other biopharma companies see the ASAP certification route as too onerous in terms of the demands on their alliance managers' time, not just for the initial certification but also for ongoing renewal. They prefer to instead operate their own internal training and development programs, which are more time efficient and customized for their own needs.

What seems to have the most powerful developmental impact on new alliance managers is hooking them into the community of existing alliance managers, so that they have experienced people to draw upon when needed. Pairing new alliance managers with more experienced ones who act as mentors or coaches works well.

The Value of an Alliance Manager

Although they arrived on the scene relatively recently, alliance managers have proven their value in partnerships. By focusing on the relational aspects of the collaboration, the alliance manager frees the project leader to focus on the scientific work and enables the project to progress by resolving collaborative issues as they arise. She or he also ensures the continued organizational support by networking across both organizations to ensure the partnership remains visible and its importance well understood. Increasingly, the question is not whether to have an alliance manager, but how you can afford not to.

Part C: Trends Looking Forward

Over the three chapters of Part C, we highlight some important trends with respect to collaboration across the biopharma R&D ecosystem. Although our primary context is bilateral R&D partnerships, these trends are also relevant to multilateral consortia and other forms of collaboration inspired by the open innovation movement.

Chapter 10 looks at the partnering-related functions that many large multinational pharma companies have made significant efforts to upgrade over the past few years. Having recognized that partnerships are now part of their daily business, these companies have sought to establish significant corporate alliance management functions, institutionalize alliance management practices, and reshape the paradigm of innovation scouting from deal sourcing to relationship building and networking.

Chapter 11 looks at the increasingly direct role played by academia and nonprofit organizations in biopharma R&D. We illustrate this developing trend by describing two models being adopted in drug discovery, namely industry-academic co-discovery alliances and nonprofit drug discovery organizations.

Chapter 12 looks at how a growing number of players in the biopharma R&D ecosystem are evolving to become networked R&D organizations that excel at partnering.

Chapter 10
Trends in Big Pharma Partnering

Recognizing that partnerships have become part of their daily business, big pharmas are investing to incorporate partnering into their existing business models. Goliath organizations are adapting to embrace networked R&D in two different ways. First, many large multinationals have built significant corporate alliance management groups with dedicated resources to support their portfolio of collaborations. In some cases, these groups are proactively institutionalizing common alliance management practices for everyone involved in collaborations across their organizations. Second, and in parallel, a small but growing number of Goliath organizations are shifting their paradigm of **innovation scouting**—finding and initiating new collaborative innovation projects—from the traditional approach of deal sourcing to networking and relationship building.

In this chapter, we look more closely at how these two themes are developing as the big pharmas transition to a new model of externalized, networked R&D.

Corporate Alliance Management Groups

Corporate alliance management groups are set up to support collaborative innovation. Many professional alliance managers in big pharmas are part of corporate alliance management groups, which manage their companies' entire portfolio of alliances. Our discussion, which focuses on helping David organizations better understand their Goliath partners, will look at:

- How the larger pharma companies determine which partnerships merit dedicated corporate alliance management resources.
- What the roles and responsibilities of corporate alliance management groups are.
- How these groups are organized and assessed.

A more detailed analysis of large pharma corporate alliance management functions is beyond the scope of this book.[1]

Allocating Corporate Alliance Management Resources

The typical big pharma may have several hundred active partnerships in just the R&D arena alone. At this level of size and complexity, it is simply impractical to deploy a dedicated alliance manager for each partnership. In order to ensure that every project gets the support it needs, companies generally segment the portfolio of partnerships and provide a different levels of support by segment.

Typical segmentation criteria incorporate three dimensions:

- *Financial impact/risk*—likely financial return and impact on the company's shareholder value.
- *Reputational impact/risk*—likely impact on industrywide reputation, regulator or payer perception, and the company's wider public image.
- *Complexity*—as determined by a combination of factors, including:
  - The nature of the scientific problem—has this the type of scientific problem been solved before?—and the range of different scientific disciplines involved in its solution.
  - The extent and frequency of interactive discussions across multiple subteams compounded by the geographic spread of participants' locations.
  - The number of collaborating organizations—is the partnership a bilateral or trilateral partnership or a multi-company industry consortium?

Some companies also consider strategic relevance—that is, how important the partnership is with respect to the company's corporate strategy—although this is usually already captured in the two risk/impact dimensions. The sheer size of the collaborative project, in terms of either team size or operating budget, usually does not matter; small partnerships can be very complex and come with huge financial and reputational risks and even large partnerships can be relatively routine, if they are focused on incremental innovations or operational outsourcing.

Alliances will typically be classified into three groups, based on their rating on each of these dimensions: Segment A alliances warrant full-time, dedicated alliance managers; segment B alliances receive some level of direct corporate-level alliance management support; and segment C alliances are managed via the business units and functional areas involved. In a typical top-ten big pharma with 500 or so active R&D alliances, perhaps 10–15 will fall into category A, 80–120 into category B, and the remainder will be in category C.[2] And this portfolio excludes hundreds more pure fee-for-service arrangements with CROs.

The Roles and Responsibilities of Corporate Alliance Management Groups

Corporate alliance management groups fulfill a number of important roles for large, multinational pharma marketers. Their most strategically important role is to optimize aggregate value and risk across the entire portfolio of partnerships within their purview. Hence, portfolio management is an important preoccupation for the leaders of such groups, including the processes of segmenting partnerships according to the attention they require and ensuring that the most appropriate alliance manager is assigned to each partnership that warrants one. Since the circumstances of each partnership and of the portfolio as a whole are continuously in flux, this is an ongoing activity; decisions about which partnerships need what kind of attention and who is allocated to provide that attention must be revisited regularly.

Another facet of portfolio management is monitoring KPIs. Corporate alliance management groups typically aggregate and summarize individual project KPIs so that they can be compared across different alliances. A typical approach is to develop measures of operational progress relative to budget and timelines, scientific progress relative to milestones, and relationship quality based on periodic health check surveys and the subjective impressions of the alliance manager. These ratings are communicated within the organization using a simple format, such as an alphabet-grade ranking or a traffic-light system. In this way, they provide a quick check on the status of each project and help alliance management group leaders and senior management see when a project might be starting to go off the rails.

From an organizational point of view, the corporate alliance management group's primary role is to provide a functional home for the company's professional alliance managers. The group recruits, trains, and develops dedicated alliance managers and monitors and manages their performance. As part of its training and development role, the group will typically maintain a continuously updated repository of best practices and tools, as well as providing the enabling technology infrastructure.

The vast majority of partnerships (at least from a volume standpoint) do not have dedicated corporate alliance managers. The alliance manager role for such partnerships is filled by one or more individuals from the functional department, business unit, or geographic organization that has the most day-to-day contact with the partner. These local alliance managers may be formally designated as full-time alliance managers, or they may fill the role in parallel with their primary function as, for example, a project leader. The corporate alliance management group provides support to this broader community of local alliance managers, including essentially anyone in the organization who performs some aspect of the alliance manager role with an external collaborator. The central group is charged with making these people aware of the nature and importance of their role; inspiring them to engage fully with it; providing training, a route for sharing experience and gathering lessons learned, tools and technology enablers; and in general spreading the alliance management gospel.

Some companies also group some other important functions under the alliance management umbrella or locate them close to the alliance management group. For example, the innovation scouting function might be part of the corporate alliance management group. Given the relationship building and corporate branding aspects that are beginning to dominate modern scouting, domiciling such professionals in the same group as the organization's best alliance managers makes a lot of sense.

Transactions and contracting professionals may also find themselves housed, organizationally and physically, with the alliance management group. This makes sense too, as good partnership design can greatly improve the odds of valuable outcomes emerging from the collaboration, and the early involvement of an experienced alliance manager in a partnership can ease the transition from negotiation to execution.

Organization and Assessment of Corporate Alliance Management Groups

The mission parameters for the corporate alliance management group (or groups, depending on the size and complexity of the organization) will depend on the corporation's business strategy and strategic priorities, as well as the number and nature of the partnerships the group oversees. The mission will be defined by a number of key decisions, including:

- Whether to maintain single or multiple corporate alliance management groups; it is not uncommon to split the mandate at the clinical PoC value inflection point, as the requirements and working style for research and early development are somewhat different from those for late-stage development, commercialization, and marketing.
- The relative split of the group's efforts between providing direct intervention and acting as a center of excellence supporting the community of local alliance managers across the organization.
- The scale, budget, and performance metrics for the group.

Once these parameters have been established, the leadership of the alliance management group can make a number of decisions with respect to the group's operating model, including:

- Whether to have only fully dedicated alliance managers or to allow for alliance managers to take on other roles, such as in scouting, due diligence, or another function.
- Where to locate the group's people: close to the partners they work with; or close to those parts of the internal organization most involved in their partnerships; or some combination of the two.
- How to organize the group's reporting lines, for instance, by therapeutic area, by type of collaboration (R&D stage, bilateral versus consortia), or by geographic location.

Since the alliance management group represents a corporate investment, it must demonstrate a tangible return on resources invested. In this context, what is important is the performance of the overall portfolio of partnerships, with greater focus on those that are high priority or strategically important. One frequently used approach is to regularly generate a dashboard of macro-level KPIs that aggregate the more-detailed individual project KPIs; these reports typically distinguish between the different segments of the partnership portfolio and are often color-coded for visual effect. In addition, diagrams that visualize the spread of resources invested or strategic relevance across the different segments are also helpful. These reports are provided to corporate management to demonstrate progress and help them monitor the portfolio in the context of the company's overall strategy.

The Institutionalization of Alliance Management Processes and Practices

In some cases, large pharmas are institutionalizing alliance management throughout their organizations by implementing common processes, shared best practices, and standardized training for all personnel who manage alliance relationships and contribute to the overall alliance management effort—not just formally assigned alliance managers. This move is a natural outgrowth of the industry's implementation of cross-functional process management as a means to operationalize global matrix structures. Essentially, these companies are treating external partnerships as the next level of the matrix organizations that they already successfully operate. As a pharma senior executive (to whom the corporate alliance management group reports) said to me, "Our organization needs to learn to matrix effectively with outside people."

The Expanding Role of the Corporate Alliance Management Group

An increasing number of corporate alliance management groups are seeing their role expand. From their original mission as support for the community of local alliance managers, they are evolving into centers of excellence and community hubs for anyone in the organization involved in alliance management activities, promoting both awareness of and the skills and tools needed for effective alliance management across the organization.

Such centers of excellence aim to ensure that all alliances are managed according to a consistent set of principles, including the less strategic or more functional and local partnerships that might receive less direct corporate attention. Their roles include:

- Nurturing the broader network of people who are involved in managing alliance relationships day-to-day, regardless of their formal reporting lines.
- Capturing, documenting, and curating alliance management processes, practices, and tools for the benefit of all network members.
- Providing training, guidance, and technology tools to network members.

These centers of excellence are proliferating. For instance, Takeda Pharmaceuticals was awarded ASAP's 2015 Alliance Program Excellence Award for building just such a capability:

> Takeda Pharmaceuticals received the award for the creation of its progressive Center of Excellence (COE) to reach more broadly across functions and geographies, including emerging markets in China, South Korea, and Russia. Members can now extensively share best practices and tools for training, management, research, enhanced communication, and an online portal.[3]

Bayer HealthCare was also recognized for a similar effort:

> Bayer HealthCare received honorable mention for its significant investment into an Alliance Capability Enhancement Project to drive a partnering mindset and alliance best practices deep into the organization.[4]

By consolidating needed information and connecting alliance managers across the organization, these groups strengthen the practice of alliance management and ensure collaborative projects are managed as effectively as possible to ensure maximum value capture.

Challenges and Limitations of Institutionalizing Alliance Management Processes

While spreading consistent practices, tools, and processes across the organization is an obvious path forward for a large corporation, this approach is not without its challenges and limitations. For a start, just because systematic support and help is being provided does not mean that people actually want it! Apathy and passive resistance can be a problem, as some managers and scientists in traditional pharmaceutical companies do not yet recognize that they need help working with outside partners, much less have the appetite to ask for it. And the alliance management group's portfolio management role often does not win it friends across the organization, especially among those whose partnerships are strategically deprioritized or whose internal projects are put on hold or terminated to be replaced by partnered projects.

The lack of understanding may extend to top management, even when partnering is a stated priority for the company. Some of the alliance managers I spoke to expressed concerns that their executive leaders did not fully appreciate the complexities and challenges of alliances; several echoed similar sentiments as these:

> Senior management are committed to alliances and value the benefits they bring, but they don't yet understand the true cost having these alliances.

> Our top management does not recognize that alliances need a lot of special attention. Alliance management training is a good idea for senior people as well!

Furthermore, alliance management is not an operational activity in the traditional sense. Implementing common practices, processes, metrics, and tools makes sense for a large company's traditional operations, and this approach should work to a certain extent for alliance management too. Nevertheless, there is a crucial difference between institutionalizing alliance management and operationalizing a global matrix organization. In the latter case, everyone works for the same corporation and that corporation can impose its own set of rules across the organization. An alliance, on the other hand, involves multiple organizations, each with its own business goals, organizational reporting structure, operating style, and culture. It is unrealistic to assume that a completely standardized set of practices, processes, metrics and tools can be imposed on every alliance, regardless of the larger partner's needs and preferences.

At the end of the day, there is no single right answer for many alliance management questions. The common platform provided by a center of excellence is merely a starting point, to be customized and adjusted for every individual alliance. I often encourage people I work with to speak of "good practices" rather than "best practices," in recognition that there is no one best way of managing an alliance, only a number of good practices that have worked in historical partnerships that can be further adapted to fit the specific circumstances of each new partnership.

Innovation Scouting as Networking and Relationship Building

In parallel with, yet separate from, the growing popularity of corporate alliance management groups, some large pharmas are also changing the way they conduct innovation scouting—finding and initiating new collaborative innovation projects. For biopharma companies seeking to collaborate to create new therapeutics and diagnostics in their therapeutic focus areas, there is now an ever-growing number and diversity of potential partners, as well as an increasing number of precompetitive research and innovation consortia. In this context, a new approach to innovation scouting is taking hold, one that sees scouting as relationship building and networking rather than as deal sourcing.

From Deal Sourcing to Relationship Building and Networking

Historically, innovation scouting was essentially a deal sourcing activity. Sellers developed non-confidential presentations and other materials describing the assets or capabilities they wished to partner, which they then announced, inviting prospective buyers to get in touch. Buyers, in turn, would announce the kinds of assets and capabilities they sought, inviting prospective sellers to get in touch. Both sides would also make contact at partnering conferences. For the buyers, this often led to compressed negotiation timelines, auction situations, and transactional relationships with prospective partners.

Recently, a new paradigm has begun to emerge, facilitated by the growing focus on geographic bioclusters. An increasing number of forward-looking companies have realized that to select the best partners and enter into the most productive partnerships, they need to identify and engage prospective collaborators and their capabilities earlier in the process. With this in mind, these companies have begun to deploy dedicated resources to:

- Build early awareness of developing assets, scientific capabilities, or new therapeutic ideas before they mature and become available subsequently in an expensive and time-consuming auction.
- Establish relationships with prospective partners, build trust, and differentiate one's own company as a valued partner by highlighting its unique characteristics.
- Learn more about their prospective partners' technical strengths, missing competencies, underlying goals, and business cultures to facilitate the eventual creation of win-win partnership agreements that are easier to close and more likely to enable a successful execution.

These aims are difficult, perhaps impossible, to achieve based on published information and brief meetings at partnering conferences. A much more effective method is to network intensively across the biocluster, establish person-to-person relationships, gather on-the-ground intelligence, and brand one's company with a human face.

This new style of innovation scouting is being separated in many organizations from the more traditional business development and transactions activity, which remains the purview of professionals skilled in negotiation and deal structuring. Whereas innovation scouting is now increasingly being carried out by networking professionals—scientifically oriented individuals with strong people skills tasked with identifying, learning about, and establishing relationships with prospective collaborators.

The importance of the human element in this new approach cannot be overemphasized. Many academic research groups and small biotechs have come to realize that they have a lot of partnering options—David organizations with desirable new ideas and technologies do not simply seek Goliath partners with money, but rather look for partners they feel they can work well with to achieve successful outcomes. Thus, an important element of Goliath's innovation scouting today is branding oneself as a good collaborator with smaller organizations. That impression is strongly shaped by the people who make the initial contact.

When this relationship-building process is successful, it leads to strong links between the new partner and the scout. This may make it advantageous for the scouting professional to remain involved with the partnership after the deal is signed, especially in collaborations involving a small number of key individuals. Sometimes, the scouting professional will continue to provide relationship management support in tandem with the alliance manager, or she or he may even become the alliance manager.

At the time of writing (mid-2015), not every large pharma conducts scouting in this manner, but the trend seems to be gathering momentum. One of the leaders in this approach is the Johnson & Johnson Innovation Center in London, a dedicated group that combines scouting and networking activity with supporting services for bioscience entrepreneurs and scientists working on innovative technologies and product ideas.[5]

Case Study—Johnson & Johnson Innovation Center

The Johnson & Johnson (J&J) Innovation Centers were launched in early 2013, with three opening within a few months of each other, in Boston, Massachusetts; the San Francisco Bay Area in

California; and London, followed by an Asia Pacific Center, in Shanghai at the end of 2014. The primary purpose of the centers is to find and secure early-stage innovations for all of J&J's businesses in pharmaceuticals, medical devices, diagnostics, and consumer health. The aim itself is not unusual; what makes the centers noteworthy is the way they accomplish it and the positive impact their approach has on their surrounding bioscience research ecosystems. We will describe in this case study what the London center does to secure innovative new medicines for J&J's pharmaceuticals business; the approach is similar in the other business and geographic areas. Keep in mind that, like all case studies, this one is meant to highlight general features; the specific details of dedicated scouting and networking groups will vary—here, again, there is no one best way.

The London team's activities revolve around eight defined areas—five therapeutic areas in pharmaceuticals (cardiovascular, immunology, neuroscience, oncology, infectious diseases & vaccines), plus diagnostics, orthopedics, and consumer products. Activity in each of these areas is driven by a therapeutic area or business lead. These eight key individuals are supported by a number of scientific specialists plus professionals in business development, finance, legal, communications, and project management, as well as two representatives from JJDC, J&J's in-house venture capital arm. In total, the center hosts a staff of approximately thirty people.

The office layout is collaboration themed, exuding warmth and openness. There are no private offices, and the space is punctuated by glass-enclosed meeting rooms equipped with virtual-working technology and communal spaces for relaxed, informal conversations. The thinking is to consolidate all deal-making capabilities in one place, and to have an open and welcoming front door into the complex J&J corporate behemoth for prospective partners.

While the operational head of the innovation center reports to J&J's Chief Scientific Officer, each of the leads reports to the relevant business area—for instance, the neuroscience lead reports to the neuroscience therapy area in Janssen Pharmaceuticals (J&J's pharmaceuticals division). Each of the leads is very focused, looking for innovations that could eventually become specific types of products for his or her area. In pharmaceuticals, each therapeutic area lead has a clear target, not just for specific diseases but also for kinds of products. Those targets are usually high impact, as explained by Immunology Lead Louise Jopling:

> We're focused on psoriasis, rheumatoid arthritis, inflammatory bowel disease, and severe asthma/COPD. Everything we do in my area needs to align with these diseases and the relevant product strategies. We want to go from systemically treating the chronic long-term inflammation to targeted delivery, treating earlier, and other approaches that would be transformative compared to the current treatment paradigm.

The underlying philosophy of the innovation center is to source and then advance early-stage innovations until they can be taken over by one of the J&J businesses. The innovation center is not just shopping for innovations—it is also nurturing them to completion.

The company's approach for doing so exhibits some unusual features, before, during, and after the deal making. Some opportunities do appear that are immediately ready for deal making. As a rule, though, the leads aim to get involved with prospective partners much earlier than the traditional business development process would kick in. They are the first point of contact for a developing partnership, and they work to build long-term relationships with the prospects. Occasionally, this approach can lead to some at-risk investment of time and money, as Transactions Lead Roger Bone explains:

> We're trying to put in place a different kind of relationship. For some companies that we really like, we may not do a deal straightaway, as what they're working on hasn't come far enough. In this case, we might say, "Let's work together, let's see how we can help each other." We offer scientific and business advice in terms of what to think about; we might even pay for experiments that we think are crucial to be done. We suggest who might be the right scientific consultant to help them, how to design the next experiment, and so on. By developing a relationship and staying close to the company, we can find out, step by step, the right information that we will need to eventually make a big partnering decision down the line.

To cultivate ideas for the kind of transformative products that they target, leads network extensively across the biocluster, connecting players who otherwise might never have met in order to stimulate and develop ideas, well before the stage when anything partnerable might emerge. They also network proactively to extend the capabilities of their partners in projects they are helping to advance, as Dr. Jopling explains:

> We build specific networks to do certain things. For example, we connected two academics from different fields in separate institutions who had been working on different aspects of what we perceived to be the same therapeutic opportunity. They would not have met otherwise, but now they are writing a grant application together. This may never turn into a deal for us, but it's part of our contribution to the immunology community.
>
> What we look at is what kind of product will offer a true innovation in patient care and how do we get at that. There may not be someone working on that, we just have to piece it together!

> We put together a network of KOLs with different translational models that extended the capabilities of some of our joint projects by enabling the testing in parallel of multiple potential indications. When it makes sense, we can also hook capabilities from various J&J R&D sites into these kinds of networks as well.

When the time comes to do a deal, the innovation center is flexible in terms of the kind of deal it puts together with early-stage partners. There is a clear focus on understanding the prospective partner's specific circumstances and crafting a customized deal structure that is attractive for both sides. In general, the innovation center team believes the best way to advance partnered early-stage opportunities is to leave the projects operating externally at the beginning, bringing to the party only what J&J has strong expertise in, as needed, until the project reaches the right stage to transition into one of their corporate businesses. Dr. Bone articulates the thinking behind this approach:

> When we internalize partners' projects too early, our people can spend a lot of time addressing perceived risk while coming up the tech transfer curve, adding extra work and costs to the program without necessarily adding a lot of extra value. If we structure our deal so that our partner can move their program rapidly under their day-to-day control, the cost is likely to be lower and they are likely to get faster to a very informative decision point whereupon we can decide that it is the time to really put in our own resources.

This philosophy can lead to some flexible deal structures, as Dr. Bone explains:

> In one case, we ended up with an option for a worldwide license that left the biotech in control of their asset and continuing to progress it downstream to a point where we felt this was the furthest they could take it on their own. The

> upfront and milestones were designed to meet the financial needs of the biotech to get to that option point. If we choose not to exercise our option at that point, they keep the asset and we walk away. So the option forces us to make a decision at a point where we know enough to fully commit.

Another unusual feature of the innovation center's approach is that the partnership continues to be managed by the innovation center after the deal is signed, instead of (as in most companies) being transitioned to one of the internal R&D groups. The lead who brought the deal in stays on as the J&J project champion for that partnership until clinical PoC is achieved, whether in a formal role on the advisory board or project team or as an informal sounding board. She or he continues as the partner's key point of contact with J&J, bringing to bear other J&J resources from around the world as and when needed. This approach is in line with the innovation center philosophy of letting the partner operationally drive the project until the time is right to transition into J&J (typically at clinical PoC).

Last but not least, in addition to the therapeutic area–driven networking, the innovation centers conduct other activities that contribute to their regions' bioscience communities. For example, they sponsor a business plan competition in which more than thirty semifinalists are selected from around 300 submissions to receive help from innovation center professionals to advance their business plans to the next level.

The innovation center approach has proved very productive. Taken together, the four innovation centers had by mid-2015 signed over 150 deals, mostly partnerships of some kind or another with a few equity investments and acquisitions, split roughly equally between academia and small companies. And these figures do not even begin to quantify the breadth of prospective collaborators that have been engaged and the depth of relationships being built.

Issues and Opportunities in the Networking and Relationship Building Paradigm

J&J's approach to a relationship-based scouting program is not based on any unique asset, advantage, or tool. In principle, anyone could do it. However, doing it well is not so easy, and while the J&J initiative seems to have made an excellent start, the true test for J&J and for others trying similar approaches is whether the investment pays off in high-impact products eventually reaching the market. Not every company adopting a networking and relationship building approach to innovation scouting will do it in the same way J&J has, but there are some common issues and opportunities for any company going down this route.

A critical success factor in any relationship-building program is the people. J&J's leads are highly knowledgeable, experienced individuals who might more typically be driving major scientific programs. This experience allows them to integrate into the local bioscience community, make the initial contacts, and engage in peer-to-peer discussions with scientists and leading-edge innovators—sometimes for months before the topic of a deal is even broached. The leads are selected for both their scientific credibility and their aptitude for networking, listening, open-minded discussion, and relationship building, not a combination of attributes that is easy to find among top-tier scientists. They also must have had sufficient project leadership experience to serve as capable project champions and coaches after a deal is struck. The supporting business development, finance, and legal professionals must also be extraordinarily qualified; they will need to craft customized nonstandard deals, thinking creatively about how to meet both J&J's needs and those of the partner.

Besides technical expertise and communication skills, innovation scouts and supporting personnel in this paradigm also must have a deep-seated belief that this is the right way to work—they must be willing to fully embrace a cooperative approach that is profoundly different from the historical behaviors of many biopharmas, which were founded on a transactional, us-versus-them view.

A key hurdle for anyone trying to get an initiative like this off the ground is justifying the investment. Beyond the nominal financial cost of the office facilities and salaries is the opportunity cost of assembling all of these handpicked people and socializing them to interact with the external ecosystem in a particular way. There is a lot of "give first to get later" in this kind of scouting model—networking, building relationships, and providing assistance without any guarantee of forthcoming deals and certainly no promise of exclusivity before a deal is signed, trusting that openness and generosity will be reciprocated when it comes time for a prospect to find a partner. Of course, operating in this way increases the company's chances of finding the best opportunities before competitors and more importantly, of having a better understanding of the scientific domain before making really big financial commitments in later-stage R&D. Nevertheless, this path requires a significant degree of longer-term thinking and senior management commitment.

In the end, a relationship-building approach to scouting is as much about culture as about organizational imperatives. The level of commitment required, long before any promise of return can reasonably be made, speaks to an organization-wide belief in the value of not just of collaborations, but of relationships.

Chapter Notes

[1] See, for instance, J. Twombly and J. Shuman, "Designing the Enterprise Capability for Managing Collaborative Relationships," *The Rhythm of Business*, August 1, 2011, http://rhythmofbusiness.com/articles/2011/8/1/designing-the-enterprise-capability-for-managing-collaborati.html.

[2] Author's estimates based on informal conversations with industry alliance managers in 2014 and 2015.

[3] Cynthia Hanson, "What Leads to Alliance Excellence? A Q&A Session with the 2015 ASAP Alliance Excellence Award Winners," *ASAP Blog*, March 4, 2015, http://www.strategic-alliances.org/blogpost/1143942/210406/What-Leads-to-Alliance-Excellence-A-Q-A-Session-with-the-2015-ASAP-Alliance-Excellence-Award-Winners.

[4] Hanson, "What Leads to Alliance Excellence?" (2015).

[5] I would like to express my thanks to Louise Jopling (Director of Immunology Scientific Innovation, Johnson & Johnson Innovation), Roger Bone (Vice President Transactions, Johnson & Johnson Innovation), and Ellen Rose (previously Communications & External Affairs Leader, Johnson & Johnson Innovation) for taking the time to tell me more about the Johnson & Johnson Innovation Center concept.

Chapter 11
The Rise of Nonprofit R&D: Case Studies in Drug Discovery

Academic and nonprofit organizations have always contributed to the discovery and development of new drugs. Historically, academia has concentrated on teaching and on conducting basic research into the underlying nature of disease causes and progression, or of certain classes of proteins or chemical compounds that might have medicinal properties. Academic medical institutions have also conducted clinical trials of new and existing drug compounds to develop a better understanding of how best to treat patients. All of the findings from these activities are typically then published for the benefit of everyone. Nonprofit organizations, whether funded by government agencies or private foundations, either replicated the academic model by setting up their own nonprofit institutes for research and higher learning or supported such work through grants to academic groups at universities and institutes.

Over the past decade, however, we have seen an increasing number of academic institutions and nonprofit organizations playing a more direct role in the biopharma R&D value chain, driving and managing some of the R&D activities and participating in the ownership of the resulting new drug compounds. At this writing, these proactive organizations represent a minority, but the momentum they have created is starting to have an impact; we will likely see in the future more and deeper strategic partnerships between academic and nonprofit researchers with commercial organizations.

The motivations of these researchers vary. Some are altruistic, seeking to promote R&D to identify treatments for diseases that are extremely challenging, such as cancer, dementia, or cystic fibrosis, or diseases that have been neglected by big pharma, such as those prevalent in less-developed countries. Some universities have more pragmatic goals, seeking to secure future funding by exploiting their ownership in the IP their researchers generate. Other universities have been encouraged by their state funders to contribute more to applied research and social well-being.

In this chapter, we will explore this developing trend and describe two models that are increasingly integrating these noncommercial players into the drug discovery domain—industry-academic co-discovery alliances and nonprofit drug discovery organizations.

Industry-Academic Co-Discovery Alliances

Strategic collaborations between biopharma companies and academic institutions are a growing phenomenon. These partnerships are essentially co-discovery partnerships in which the two organizations work together to innovate new medicines. For example, witness these recent strategic alliances:

- The University of Oxford and UCB initiated an alliance in 2012 to pursue "innovative biomedical research that would help deliver transformative new therapies for patients with high unmet clinical needs. The scientific focus for the Alliance is in immunology and neuroscience and [it] has adopted a collaborative approach to progressing research through joint working and staff exchanges."[1]
- University College London and Eisai initiated an alliance at the end of 2012 that involves researchers from both organizations working together to "investigate radical new ways of treating neurological diseases such as Alzheimer's, Parkinson's and other related disorders" and "identify and validate novel drug targets, develop new therapeutics and evaluate them in proof-of-concept clinical trials."[2]
- The German Cancer Research Center (Deutsches Krebsforschungszentrum, DKFZ) and Bayer HealthCare initiated an alliance in 2009 and renewed it in 2014 for the purpose of "jointly developing novel therapeutic options for cancer patients."[3]

Each such alliance is unique in its own way, but in general, they go significantly beyond the traditional academic-industry collaboration models of industry-sponsored basic research or fee-for-service work. Some of the distinguishing features of these second-generation partnerships include:

- An umbrella alliance comprising multiple collaborative projects across several years, involving multiple academic laboratories and their **principal investigators**. In the traditional model, each laboratory would have its own individual arrangement with the biopharma sponsor.

- A joint goal to discover new medicines for a particular group of diseases, rather than just expanding the scientific knowledge base about those diseases.
- Direct involvement by academic researchers as operational players in collaborative, early-stage drug discovery projects that are set up and managed to industry standards rather than as academic research projects.
- Academic researchers working in close cooperation with industry scientists, with whom they interact frequently rather than operating at arm's length as in the traditional model.

The alliance between the DKFZ and Bayer HealthCare offers an illustration of the potential benefits of this alliance and suggests how these arrangements typically operate.[4] Like all case studies, it is meant to highlight certain general features; keep in mind that the specific details of other alliances will differ.

Case Study: The DKFZ–Bayer Alliance

The DKFZ–Bayer alliance was consummated in 2009, some two years after an informal conversation between the DKFZ's chairman and Bayer's head of drug discovery, which evolved into detailed negotiations between two small senior-level teams from each side and eventually into a five-year umbrella agreement. The agreement was amended in 2013 to establish a joint immunotherapy laboratory staffed by scientists from both parties, working side by side. In February 2014, after a joint investment over the previous five years of more than €10 million, the two parties implemented a new, comprehensive five-year partnership. To quote the formal press release, "Bayer and the DKFZ will together invest up to 30 million Euros into their collaboration over the next five years to address the high medical need in cancer treatment and diagnosis." The DKFZ's CEO commented that the agreement would enable the partners to "build on the excellent results of [the DKFZ's] basic research and transfer them to the clinic."[5]

The DKFZ has more than 3,000 employees, including more than 1,000 scientists at its base in Heidelberg, organized into a large number of different research groups and laboratories. The arrangement with Bayer is not exclusive—no one from the DKFZ is required to work within the alliance—but the existence of an umbrella agreement and a well-understood grant application process means that any scientist looking for a potential industry collaborator is likely to consider Bayer as an option. And anyone at the DKFZ can come up with an idea for a joint project with Bayer.

Projects are selected and initiated through a simple process. Short project idea summaries, just one to three pages long, go to a joint committee for review. If the committee deems an idea interesting, a DKFZ principal investigator and a Bayer project champion are assigned to develop a full proposal. Once they are approved, most projects start with a dedicated postdoc and a technician working under the supervision of the DKFZ principal investigator at the DKFZ's site in Heidelberg. Depending on the project, Bayer people may or may not be operationally involved at the very early stages. As a project advances, Bayer personnel, from assay development, screening, medicinal chemistry, antibody optimization, and other specialties, are increasingly involved on a day-to-day basis and some of the work is conducted at Bayer's headquarters in Berlin, its US Innovation Center in San Francisco, and elsewhere. At this stage, the project team members are distributed between the DKFZ's site in Heidelberg and at least one, and sometimes several, Bayer sites. Project meetings take place monthly; at least two (and more usually three or four) meetings each year are held face to face rather than by videoconference or teleconference.

An exception to these dispersed physical working arrangements is the new joint immunotherapy laboratory at Germany's

National Center for Tumor Diseases in Heidelberg, at which DKFZ and Bayer personnel work side by side.[6] As of mid-2015, this group comprised eight full-time scientists funded by the joint alliance budget plus another four funded solely by Bayer working together on four projects, one of which is already approaching the end of the lead optimization stage. The plan is to increase the staff size and expand the number of concurrently running projects to seven, with the aim of taking at least one or two projects into preclinical development.

Historically, therapeutic projects at the DKFZ ended at the drug target validation stage. The alliance with Bayer aims to take projects further under the auspices of the alliance, with formal goals in the second agreement including the aim to create a strong portfolio of projects that could eventually lead to a small number of Phase I clinical programs. So while projects often start with the aim of validating unprecedented targets, successful efforts will continue into the later stages of drug discovery, with both parties working together to identify potential chemical or antibody molecules, better understand the biological mode of action, and identify relevant biomarkers. The new joint laboratory aims to continue further to deliver projects to the preclinical development stage.

All the joint projects in the alliance are proposed, designed, and managed to industry standards, with a focus on a clear work plan, defined milestones, and established go/no-go criteria—all elements not common to typical academic research projects. Dr. Ruth Wellenreuther, the DKFZ's dedicated alliance manager for the Bayer partnership, noted:

> Our projects will be fully integrated into the Bayer pipeline if licensed. So they need to be managed like industry projects to the same standards, otherwise we cannot be competitive with Bayer's internal projects. The worst thing for a DKFZ scientist is going on to complete a joint project successfully, having it

licensed to Bayer, and then seeing it being neglected or not worked on owing to it being a low priority at Bayer.

The joint projects are governed via a two-level committee structure. JRCs (one for the joint laboratory and one for other joint projects) monitor the project teams' progress. The review committees, which are made up of three voting members from each side plus a number of permanent non-voting members, meet monthly. Above the two review committees, an overall JSC meets quarterly to make funding decisions; its membership is also comprised of three voting members from each side plus additional non-voting members, including both parties' alliance managers. The budget for the alliance is contractually segregated and under the control of the JSC, which has complete authority to decide how it is allocated, regardless of the current financial priorities in either of the parent organizations.

Academic publication is an important activity at most non-commercial research institutions, and the DKFZ is no different. Every joint project PI is encouraged to create a publication strategy in agreement with Bayer at the outset. The strategy could vary widely depending on nature of the individual project—whether it is for a *de novo* target or an already published target, whether it is in a competitive field or an altogether new field, and so on. Bayer has openly declared that it is also interested in joint publication, subject to the right timing—regular publication is a declared strategic goal in the alliance. If the bare bones of a publication strategy for a particular project cannot be agreed on up-front, the DKFZ alliance manager will politely suggest that the PI not proceed with a joint project. In all cases, as part of the overarching alliance agreement, the publication of results must be approved by Bayer. The Bayer team has four weeks to respond after receiving a draft manuscript and may suggest changes to the manuscript. Alternately, Bayer can opt to make a patent application, in which case the publication may be delayed for a further period of some months while the patent application is prepared and filed.

Once each major stage of the project is finalized and the project report is submitted to the JSC, Bayer has a defined period in which to notify the DKFZ that it wishes to exercise its option to in-license the project. If the option is not exercised within the allowed time, the results are still jointly owned, but the DKFZ can request a transfer of IP rights to allow the institute to develop the project further with a different partner. This has actually happened in at least one case.

Owing to the newness of this way of working and the sheer scale and diversity of the alliance, both Bayer and the DKFZ have assigned dedicated alliance managers. Working together, these two individuals provide templates and guidance for new project proposals, help the DKFZ principal investigators and the Bayer project champions jointly define milestones and go/no-go criteria, facilitate agreement on publication strategies and project reporting arrangements at the outset of new projects, and convene project kickoff meetings. Although they are usually not involved in the monthly project team meetings, they are important non-voting participants in the review and steering committees.

Through the end of the first five-year agreement in early 2014, twenty-eight joint projects had been initiated. Of the twenty that were still ongoing at the initiation of the new alliance, twelve had moved into the compound screening stage; two of these had gone even further and identified candidate drugs while another three had been exclusively licensed by Bayer.

Given these statistics, it is not surprising that both sides have been very happy with this new way of working together, to the extent that the partnership was renewed with triple its original budget and the addition of a joint laboratory. At the individual level, the senior scientists who lead the laboratory groups are also highly appreciative of the arrangement, as articulated by Dr. Wellenreuther:

> Our scientists have opportunity to translate their ideas to a real healthcare application. They get a lot of support in kind from Bayer—small molecule screening, computational chemistry, antibody libraries, etc. The main motivation for our PIs who have embraced the joint projects is not the funding but to see their ideas going well into the direction of reaching the patient.
>
> Our scientists also learn a lot about how the pharma industry looks at certain drug targets and runs projects. They get to learn about the process to create a new drug; most of this is through learning by doing with their Bayer project colleagues, although we have also organized some training sessions such as a drug discovery seminar series. And they also see what industry looks for, including some of them being invited as guests to internal Bayer portfolio review meetings to hear how the projects they initiated are discussed.

Comments from some of the DKFZ principal investigators involved in the joint projects also endorse the wider benefits of the alliance:

> Our monthly joint team teleconference was not just about the project but also included discussion of emerging developments in the field, recent literature and its implications, etc. Very helpful and it happened naturally.
>
> We had the possibility to jointly design the project, with work being done by both sides. They were open to sharing their technologies such as HTS [high-throughput screening]. A very fruitful collaboration—our Bayer discussion partners changed as the project progressed, we gained a lot of specialist know-how from them and they learnt a lot from us too.
>
> My advice to other PIs considering another collaborative project like this is to DO IT!

Issues and Opportunities with Industry-Academic Co-Discovery Alliances

While the benefits of these kinds of second-generation industry-academic alliances are clear, they also have issues and potential downsides that need to be managed. Alignment between industry and academia is inherently difficult, owing to significantly different belief systems and research philosophies. For example, they differ radically in their approach to the question of publication. Academic career paths are determined by publications. In particular, postdocs who are just starting their careers will be most concerned about publication constraints. On the other hand, companies would often prefer to keep results confidential until a product reaches the market. Agreeing on a publication strategy up-front helps, of course, but it will still be seen as a compromise in the eyes of many academics; one PI I interviewed told me that in one extreme case, it took a year of discussion and negotiation before he was allowed to publish the structure of a compound. This is a critical issue for academic researchers, as another interviewee told me: "While the top leadership of academic organizations may want to bring drug candidates into the clinic, the incentive systems in academic institutions push in the direction of publication, so this paradox needs to be addressed."

Similarly, while companies might prefer exclusivity in their relationships with academic laboratories, it is important for credibility with the academic community to forego insisting on it, especially since these alliances are at the level of the institution, not the lab. Those laboratory heads who wish to participate in the alliance can opt in, but no one should feel pressured to do so.

The need to run co-discovery projects according to industry standards also brings a number of challenges. First, the very structured approach, with milestones, go/no-go criteria, reporting requirements, and a singular focus, is not native to academic researchers, and it may take a while for them to get used to it.

That said, those who have participated in these alliances do recognize the benefits of this approach. The PIs I interviewed pointed out both the benefits and the stresses of acclimating to it:

> Tight milestones, managed timelines and clear go/no-go criteria can be very helpful, but they are also hard at first for us academics to operate with. There is also less liberty to change the scope and pursue interests in side findings.

> It can feel quite stressful initially with the added discussion, communication and reporting workload.

Second, industry projects carry inherently more uncertainty and are subject to factors beyond the visibility of the academic principal investigators. Unlike a traditional grant-funded project with a fixed duration, industry projects can be canceled for any of a number of reasons at the next steering committee review. Industry researchers are used to this kind of portfolio management approach, but it can very disconcerting for academics, as my interviewees noted:

> What gets me are the binary decisions at every major go/no-go review and the resulting uncertainty. As academics, we plan for two to five years, that's how long we can fund postdocs and PhD students for, whereas an industry joint project with a two- or three-year planned timeline may not last that long ... it could fail for technical reasons, but it could also fail for intellectual property reasons if a competitor has filed a patent application. And with the next corporate restructuring initiative, the company could lose interest quickly in the area you are working on.

> Our people struggle with projects being stopped when a clinical candidate does not look viable even though to them there is still a lot of science to do and a lot of publishable discoveries to be made.

Conversely, changes in corporate internal priorities (for instance, failures in other parts of the company's portfolio) or progress by competitors often create pressure on the project champions to, for example, accelerate timelines. This, too, can cause tension with academic principal investigators, who are not used to this level of outside pressure on their work.

Resource inflexibility on the academic side can also create tension as the project endures its inevitable ups and downs. For example, the chemical structures required to modulate the drug target may prove difficult to determine, a not-uncommon scenario that can delay progress in the next phase. While the company's medicinal chemistry group deals with this challenge, what does the academic biology team do with its people? Unlike a company that can reassign people to short-term roles on other projects, academic postdocs and PhD students are funded for specific projects and they cannot easily move to other projects in other laboratories. Similarly, in the face of pressure to accelerate a project, an industry lab would likely be able to borrow personnel from another project. Academic groups cannot easily borrow postdocs from other laboratories.

One interesting approach to mitigating the resource uncertainty and inflexibility concerns is the approach taken for instance by the UCL–Eisai alliance, which maintains a small, dedicated group of scientists that can be deployed to support any project that requires it. The alliance agreement specifically allocates funding to this group to ensure every project has the personnel it needs. In a similar vein, one feature of the DKFZ-Bayer joint immunotherapy laboratory is the possibility to shift personnel across projects as and when needed.

Nonprofit Drug Discovery Organizations

Another species of collaborator that has been gaining prominence is the nonprofit drug discovery organization. While such entities have been in existence for a while, their prevalence, funding level, and visibility in the biopharma R&D ecosystem have grown significantly over the past decade.

There is a fair degree of diversity in this space. Some organizations are focused around specific diseases with high unmet needs such as Cancer Research UK. Others, such as the Drugs for Neglected Diseases initiative, seek to address areas in which commercial biopharma companies have been under-investing. Still others, such as MRC Technology, grew out of government-funded research initiatives seeking to bridge the gap between academic research and the pharmaceutical world. And yet others, such as the Dundee Drug Discovery Unit, were created within academic institutions. Some of these organizations are self-contained units with their own laboratories and a full suite of drug discovery capabilities, while others act as project initiators, funders, and managers, coordinating work at academic laboratories, service providers, and other nonprofit organizations.

All of these diverse organizations share three common characteristics:

- They initiate and drive their own projects in the drug discovery space.
- They partner with traditional academic laboratories at the front of the drug discovery process and with biopharma companies at the later stages.
- They have their own source of funding and are not fully reliant on partnership revenue.

These characteristics differentiate them from classic academic laboratories conducting grant-funded basic research and from the industry-academic alliance collaborators, which operate in tandem with industry partners. Instead, nonprofit drug discovery organizations play a role akin to that of a research-stage biotech or focused biopharma company, shaping and nurturing certain IP assets over a selected portion of the R&D value chain. But unlike their industrial counterparts, they operate a nonprofit financing model with concomitant goals and ethos.

As an example of the approach nonprofit drug discovery organizations take, we consider the case of the United Kingdom charity MRC Technology.[7] Like all case studies, this one is meant only to highlight general features; the specific details of other organizations will differ.

Case Study: MRC Technology

MRC Technology (MRCT) is a spinoff of the United Kingdom's Medical Research Council (MRC), a public-sector entity that provides grants for academic research across the biomedical spectrum. Formerly known as the MRC Collaborative Centre and then the MRC Technology Transfer Group, MRCT became a separate entity with charitable status in 2000; its charter was to handle the technology transfer needs of the MRC. Today it is, according to its website, "an independent life science medical research charity that helps bridge the gap between basic research and commercial application."[8]

MRCT provides a number of services to academic research groups in the biomedical arena (whether they are funded by MRC or not), such as evaluating their research portfolios to look for projects with commercial potential and helping them protect the IP in those projects. What we are most concerned with here, though, is their investment in developing some of these projects further, and in particular their in-house Centre for Therapeutics Discovery, which as of mid-2015 comprised approximately seventy people conducting earlier-stage drug discovery projects.

At its launch in 2000, MRCT did not have a full suite of drug discovery capabilities, only a screening facility plus a strong capability in antibody humanization based on a technology platform that it had the rights to deploy under license from the MRC. Application of this capability with various pharma partners generated fee-for-service revenues and eventually resulted in royalty streams from two blockbuster products—Tysabri (natalizumab), for multiple sclerosis and Crohn's disease, and Actemra (tocilizumab/atlizumab), for rheumatoid arthritis. More recently, two other major products reached the market with the help of MRCT's antibody humanization capabilities, resulting in further royalty streams from Entyvio (vedolizumab), for ulcerative colitis and Crohn's disease, and Keytruda (pembrolizumab), for metastatic melanoma. Over the past fifteen years, this cash flow has enabled MRCT to build up its drug discovery capabilities and fund its own portfolio of drug discovery projects. MRCT is now completely self-funded with royalties from its past projects and revenue from running partnerships.

MRCT's focus on drug discovery is succinctly encapsulated by its Director of Drug Discovery, Dr. Justin Bryans: "We span the 'valley of death' in early-stage research, the gap between what academia produces and what pharma companies prefer to start with." The starting point for MRCT's small molecule projects is usually an idea for a drug target from an academic collaborator plus some supporting experimental data from gene knockouts or cell-based experiments. Once such a target is identified, MRCT proceeds to develop the idea through several steps:

1) Develop screening assays.
2) Determine chemical starting points derived from medium-throughput screening.
3) Demonstrate that a medicinal chemistry approach is viable.
4) Develop tool compounds with good potency and selectivity.
5) Establish nonclinical proof-of-concept by putting these compounds through relevant cell-based or *in vivo* models.

The approach for biologics is similar, although the academic's starting package in this case often includes an off-the-shelf antibody or home-grown polyclonal antibody. MRCT then generates a monoclonal antibody, demonstrates its affinity, humanizes it, and puts it through the appropriate cell-based or *in vivo* models.

As is normal across the industry, the majority of these projects end up demonstrating that the original hypothesis was flawed. Unusually, however, MRCT sees this as a good thing, according to Dr. Bryans:

> We believe the negative results are by themselves a good service. We will publish that so that others won't make the same mistake and pursue that target. As a charity, that is an important thing for us to be doing; someone has to do this as it would never otherwise be picked up by the broader drug discovery community.

When the appropriate *in vitro* or *in vivo* proof-of-concept has been established, MRCT partners the project to a biopharma company that then takes it further. After this point, MRCT is no longer operationally involved, although the original academic collaborator may continue to work with the biopharma partner. At the point of partnering, in small molecule projects, MRCT usually delivers a chemical series (with corresponding tools and data) that is highly potent and selective, although with a few issues that require further optimization; for biologics, MRCT delivers a humanized antibody that could be the actual drug candidate. While a research-stage biotech would traditionally partner after gaining regulatory permission to initiate the first human trial, MRCT partners somewhat earlier. This is because, in Dr. Bryans's words, "After having done the analysis, we believe there isn't really a big inflection point in value anyway until you get to clinical proof-of-concept at Phase II."

The partnership model MRCT seeks is typically an IP transfer arrangement based on an up-front payment, contingent clinical milestone payments, and a royalty arrangement on future sales. Between 2014 and mid-2015 alone, one antibody and three small molecule discovery projects were partnered out in this way; since its inception, MRCT has been involved in eight clinical and three preclinical development-stage projects currently in the pipelines of various pharma companies.

MRCT has an attractive value proposition for the academics it partners with, especially those who want their ideas developed further but are uninterested in or simply not yet ready to create a biotech startup and pursue venture capital funding. Ideas are tested at no cost to the academic originator, who is part of the project team, sees all the data, and can influence where the project is going. And if the project is partnered out, the researcher or his or her home institution receive a share of the value generated. MRCT is also willing, where it is feasible, to provide antibodies or small molecules (usually not from the main series but perfectly adequate for the job) that academic researchers can use as tools in their own laboratories and to support future publications. In some cases, MRCT has helped seed new startup companies from its projects, for example, Heptares in 2007.

MRCT's value proposition is also attractive for biopharma companies. Namely, the organization minimizes the risk associated with new drug targets by taking ideas from academia and demonstrating their viability as treatments for diseases of interest by generating relevant evidence. When a project is partnered out, the receiving company has much higher confidence (compared to the typical academic starting point) that the project can be progressed effectively; at the same time, the company acquires an asset that is not yet fully formed and can be molded to its specific requirements.

Increasingly, MRCT has been conducting joint endeavors with biopharma companies at an earlier stage in its projects. For example it has a multi-project alliance with AstraZeneca in which the company chooses from among a set of targets that MRCT proposes, based on its academic collaborations, and then supports MRCT's work on those targets by providing free access to a large selection of AstraZeneca's compounds plus pharmacology expertise and other advice.[9] Once the targets reach a certain point in the establishment of *in vitro* or *in vivo* PoC, they will be transferred to AstraZeneca. MRCT also operates a similar alliance with Daiichi Sankyo.[10]

In addition, MRCT is part of the Dementia Consortium with Alzheimer's Research UK, Eisai, and Eli Lilly.[11] In this arrangement, the other participants provide funding and advice and MRCT applies its process to minimize the risk associated with potential dementia targets proposed to the consortium by academic researchers.

In common with many of its nonprofit drug discovery brethren, MRCT has a reliable source of funding and no short-term investor pressures, allowing it to provide an interesting proposition in the collaborative R&D ecosystem, as Dr. Bryans notes:

> At one end, we provide what the academics lack, and at the other end, we enable pharma companies to tap into academia with less up-front cost and risk. We want to be seen as a one-stop shop, where pharmas can come to us and see a very broad spectrum of projects, and the academics can come to us for a very broad spectrum of drug discovery resources and help.

Issues and Opportunities in Nonprofit Drug-Discovery Organizations

Despite the clear benefits of the model exemplified by MRCT's case, it is not so straightforward for every nonprofit institution to start its own drug discovery group. Many institutions appear to be making noises about going in this direction, but the challenges are significant—how many organizations have the will to make a truly concerted effort, invest the necessary resources to create a critical mass of people, and provide the right equipment? As the projects are initially self-funded, any new group will need a reliable source of funding, probably over and above what could be generated by concurrent fee-for-service work, until some projects generate royalties or transfer payments. That imperative could hamper other efforts by denying funds to existing academic groups that are currently being funded by some of these organizations.

Furthermore, in my experience, drug discovery is a complex endeavor that is as much an artisan skill as it is a science. It is certainly not a repeatable, cookie-cutter process—as the big pharmas found out to their detriment in the 1990s. Finding and deploying the right people is key. The only place these skills can be learned is in pharma and biotech companies that have accumulated years of experience, even the ones that have had lots of project failures—after all, the more you fail, the smarter you know about what not to do! What's needed, then, to found and operate a successful nonprofit discovery group is people with industry experience who know how to operate projects to industry standards, plus smart, capable researchers from academia who can add creativity and innovative thinking. The group culture should be an amalgam of the industrial and the academic environment. This is not an easy, or cheap, balance to achieve.

The Role of Nonprofit R&D

Nonprofit R&D organizations, including both industry-academic alliances and drug discovery organizations, fill a critical gap in the biopharma R&D ecosystem, providing a bridge between academia and industry. Whether academic researchers work alongside industry scientists in an industry project, as in an alliance, or the organization develops and feeds ideas from academia to industry, as in the nonprofit drug discovery organization, these collaborations push ideas along the pipeline toward the market. Ultimately, they provide real value, to the academic researchers looking to develop their ideas, the biopharmas looking for innovations to ensure their future, and society seeking new healthcare solutions.

Chapter Notes

1 University of Oxford Medical Sciences Division, "The UCB-Oxford Alliance: Innovation and Industry," University of Oxford Medical Sciences Division, http://www.medsci.ox.ac.uk/support-services/innovation-industry/business-development/the-ucb-oxford-alliance.

2 UCL, "Eisai Pharmaceuticals and UCL Form Drug Discovery Alliance," press release, December 13, 2012, http://www.ucl.ac.uk/news/news-articles/1212/131212-ucl-easai-pharmaceuticals-discovery-alliance.

3 Bayer HealthCare, "Bayer and German Cancer Research Center (DKFZ) in Strategic Alliance Against Cancer," press release, February 4, 2014, https://pharma.bayer.com/en/partnering/news/news-page.php/15383/2014-0041. Also available at http://www.dkfz.de/en/presse/pressemitteilungen/2014/dkfz-pm-14-06-Bayer-and-German-Cancer-Research-Center-DKFZ-in-Strategic-Alliance-Against-Cancer.php.

4 I would like to express my thanks to Dr. Ruth Wellenreuther (DKFZ's alliance manager for the alliance with Bayer) for taking the time to tell me more about the Bayer–DKFZ alliance and for arranging similar discussions with several DKFZ PIs who have participated in joint projects with Bayer. I would also like to thank Prof. Dr. Eckhard Ottow and Dr. Christoph Huwe of Bayer for pointing me toward the Bayer–DKFZ alliance, and Dr. Holger Hess-Stumpp (Bayer's alliance manager for the alliance with DKFZ) for putting me in contact with Dr. Wellenreuther.

5 Bayer, "Bayer and German Cancer Research Center (DKFZ) in Strategic Alliance Against Cancer" (2014).

[6] Joint industry-academic laboratories are becoming increasingly fashionable, as evidenced by the September 2015 announcement of the establishment of a joint laboratory by AstraZeneca's MedImmune division and Cancer Research UK where, to quote the official press release, "Cancer Research UK and MedImmune scientists will work together in the laboratory and collaborate closely to share knowledge and expertise to discover and develop novel biologics to treat and diagnose cancer." Cancer Research UK, "Cancer Research UK and MedImmune Launch Ground-Breaking Biotherapeutics Research Centre in Cambridge," press release, September 11, 2015, http://www.cancerresearchuk.org/about-us/cancer-news/press-release/2015-09-11-cancer-research-uk-and-medimmune-launch-ground-breaking-biotherapeutics-research-centre-in-cambridge.

[7] I would like to express my thanks to Dr. Justin Bryans (MRC Technology's Head of Drug Discovery) for taking the time to tell me more about MRC Technology's Centre for Therapeutics Discovery.

[8] MRC Technology, "About Us," http://www.mrctechnology.org/about-us/.

[9] MRC Technology, "MRC Technology and AstraZeneca Renew Collaboration to Identify Novel Targets for Drug Discovery Research," press release, July 3, 2014, http://www.mrctechnology.org/mrc-technology-astrazeneca-renew-collaboration-identify-novel-targets-discovery-research/.

[10] MRC Technology, "MRC Technology and Daiichi Sankyo Collaborate to Identify Novel Targets for Drug Discovery," press release, May 14, 2014, http://www.mrctechnology.org/mrc-technology-daiichi-sankyo-collaborate-identify-novel-targets-drug-discovery/.

[11] Alzheimer's Research UK, "3m Dementia Consortium Launched to Boost Dementia Drug Discovery," press release, December 10, 2013, http://www.alzheimersresearchuk.org/3m-dementia-consortium-launched-to-boost-dementia-drug-discovery/.

Chapter 12
Emergence of the Networked R&D Organization

As big pharma companies have come to see collaboration as the solution to their R&D productivity woes, partnering has become an increasingly valuable if not essential capability. Gradually, these Goliath companies, which once conducted nearly all of their R&D in-house, are evolving. Vertical integration is giving way to a plethora of collaborations that support projects at every stage of drug discovery and development. At the same time, research-stage biotechs, smaller pharmas, CROs and nonprofit organizations—the David entities—are evolving to systematically pursue multiple concurrent partnerships with both the big pharmas and their peers. They are moving from being suppliers of IP and skills to becoming major and essential collaborators as the biopharma R&D ecosystem evolves into a rich global network of partnerships. In other words, both Goliath and David are becoming **networked R&D organizations**. The romantic notion that many research-stage biotechs and smaller pharmas had in the 1990s of being the "David that slew Goliath"—birthing the next blockbuster drug and becoming the next big pharma—is increasingly being replaced by the desire to profitably participate as a full partner in the global network of biopharma R&D collaborations.

This chapter explores this evolution and considers its implications. We look at how organizations evolve as they seek to get better at partnering, a journey that leads down one of two paths—to the *partnering-savvy* organization or the *partnering-centric* one.

Evolving Toward the Networked R&D Organization: Two Paths

Biopharma R&D partnering is not a new phenomenon—both industry-academic collaborations and bilateral partnerships between companies have been going on for decades. There are probably very few established companies that are **partnering-naive**—having little or no experience of partnering—although there may still be parts of some companies that until very recently did not collaborate with outsiders. What has changed in recent years is the rapid growth in the sheer number and complexity of partnerships. Partnerships are now ubiquitous across the entire R&D value chain, from basic research into biological pathways and disease etiology all the way to product launch and commercialization. As a result, a significant level of R&D externalization is now considered the norm in many companies.

Before the rate of R&D partnering started to seriously accelerate 10–15 years ago, many companies were **partnering-tolerant**. Partnerships with other R&D organizations and service providers were seen as a practical necessity (and by some even as a necessary evil), to bring in resources or funding, add new ideas or skills, address gaps in expertise, or provide scalable capacity. When asked about the critical imperatives for managing partnerships, many R&D executives in partnering-tolerant companies would have said, "We need to ensure we get what we need from our partners, while making sure we control their use of our resources within our contractual obligations."

Hopefully, there are probably very few organizations today that are still at this stage. Many companies have evolved, becoming much smarter and more sophisticated in their partnering as they pursue, and learn from, a growing number of alliances with an increasingly diverse set of partners. In the process, as they come to terms with the new reality of operating partnerships, these companies begin to evolve in one of two alternative directions—toward being **partnering-savvy** or **partnering-centric** (Figure 12.1).

***Figure 12.1.* Evolutionary Paths to the Networked R&D Organization**

Partnering-Savvy	Partnering-Centric
Organization and operations adjusted to handle partnerships as extensions to normal business Mix of in-house and partnered projects; portfolio review ensures level playing field Corporate alliance management oversees entire partnership portfolio—dedicated alliance managers assigned to the most important alliances Alliance management = a common platform of processes and tools available to those involved in managing relationships	Partnerships integrated into daily work and embedded into the organizational culture All projects involve external collaborators, often via high-interaction partnership models Very positive feedback from partners regarding collaborative style Alliance management = a set of skills and competencies embedded into the fabric of the organization and deployed by everyone

These two flavors of networked R&D organization represent different but equally viable approaches to building an organization that excels at operating partnerships. Most organizations today are nowhere close to completing the journey, but many are clearly on the way in one of these two directions.

Partnering-Savvy Organizations

Partnering-savvy organizations see collaborating with external R&D partners as an important and permanent extension to their business model that generates a significant net positive increase in value compared to working traditionally. They know they need to partner well in order for their business to be successful. When asked about the critical imperatives for managing partnerships, many R&D executives in such organizations might say, "We need to make additional organizational adjustments and operational arrangements to work effectively and efficiently with our partners. We recognize that partnerships involve a strong measure of give and take." A partnering-savvy organization in the making can usually be recognized by the adjustments it makes to connect its R&D partnerships into its existing operating framework. These changes are captured in a number of elements, such as:

- A mixed R&D portfolio comprising both in-house and partnered projects, combined with a portfolio review process that ensures a level playing field for both internal and external efforts.
- A thriving corporate alliance management group that oversees the entire portfolio of external partnerships, deploying dedicated alliance managers for the most important alliances.
- Significant efforts to institutionalize across the whole organization a platform of common alliance management processes, practices and tools, available to all who have to manage relationships with partners.

Partnering-savvy organizations are built through systematic adjustment and addition of structures and processes that facilitate working with large numbers of external collaborators.

Many multinational pharmas are pursuing the partnering-savvy route. We have discussed at some length in Chapters 9 and

10 those elements of a partnering-savvy organization that need to be added, such as professional alliance managers, corporate alliance management functions, a common platform of alliance management processes, practices and tools across the organization, and a shift in the innovation scouting paradigm from deal sourcing to networking and relationship building.

Partnering-Centric Organizations

Where partnering-savvy organizations see partnering as a critical addition to their business model, partnering-centric organizations see external partnerships as the core essence of their business model. The internal structures, processes, and culture of the latter are all centered around partnering. Unlike partnering-savvy organizations, which partner to make their main business more effective and efficient, partnering-centric companies see effective and efficient partnering *as* their main business. When asked about the critical imperatives for managing partnerships, senior executives in such organizations might say, "We need to integrate our partners into our daily work and infuse a win-win collaborative problem-solving mentality into our culture. Everyone has a role to play in managing relationships with our collaborators."

The partnering-centric philosophy is fundamentally about how people think and behave rather than about the implementation of a different organizational structure or business process. As a result, the manifestations of an organization transitioning to a partnering-centric model are more subtle than those indicating the emergence of a partnering-savvy organization. Nevertheless, there are three tell-tale signs of a partnering-centric organization in the making:

- Every, or nearly every, R&D project and initiative involves external collaborators; while the degree of ownership may vary from one project to another, there is no distinction between in-house and external projects. The partnership

models implemented in the company's collaborations are predominantly high-interaction variants in which both sides interact and engage with each other frequently.
- David, Goliath, and peer partners with different cultures and operating processes all offer very positive feedback about the company's collaborative working style.
- Alliance management is seen as a set of skills and competencies embedded into the fabric of the organization and deployed by everyone, rather than as a platform of processes, practices and tools deployed by those with relationship management roles. Partnerships are not managed as a separate activity—they are part and parcel of the daily work.

More About Partnering-Centric Organizations

Through hard-won experience in successive partnerships, a growing band of organizations is moving toward becoming partnering-centric, with people and cultures optimized for working intensively with a diverse range of collaborators. Yet many of the organizations going in this direction may not even be conscious that they are pursuing this route—they are merely doing what seems natural for them.

To date, the majority of emerging partnering-centric organizations have not deliberately shaped their organizations to be the way they are. Instead, their culture and way of working has evolved organically through the interplay between decisions made to mitigate constraints or capture opportunities in their business, with experiences and learnings from partnerships they have been involved in. Usually, partnering-centric organizations begin from one of three scenarios:

- Smaller or medium-sized traditional pharmaceutical companies choose to implement a semi-virtual R&D model in which they over-invest compared to their peers in certain components of the R&D value chain while relying mostly on partners and service providers for other components.
- Research-stage biotechs or technology providers evolve into full-fledged product companies using a semi-virtual model for both their R&D and commercial capabilities.
- Smaller to medium-sized CROs and other service and technology providers choose a business model that relies on delivering highly customized solutions via high-interaction partnering models.

The common denominator in every case is that, out of business necessity, they have had to operate a large number of collaborations with a diverse range of partners while contending with each partner's unique business processes, working style, and culture. Furthermore, a large proportion of their people needed to get involved in the day-to-day operation of these partnerships, more often than not working with multiple partners concurrently. In true Darwinian fashion, many of the companies that prospered in this context were those that were able to foster in their people an adeptness at working collaboratively with many different partners, while retaining both their core scientific competencies and their own unique culture.

The Key Ingredients of a Partnering-Centric Organization

The partnering-centric organization has several key ingredients. First, successful partnering-centric organizations are **project-centric**. This means that:

- Most people's to-do list is driven by the projects they are directly working on or indirectly supporting, rather than by their functional departments and line managers.

- Projects are the focal point or center of gravity for decision making and resource allocation.
- While most people might have a permanent organizational home, such as a functional department or scientific discipline, they identify most strongly with the projects they are working on and see as their closest colleagues those working with them on the same projects. They are excited and motivated when they move from one project to another, as this signals new opportunities to explore.

Once a project-centric mindset has started to take hold in the organization, a partner-centric mindset is just a short step away—after all, partnerships are simply projects conducted with people from outside the company.

A second important prerequisite is a strong set of scientific, technical, or commercial competencies that their partners find valuable. You can be very good to work with, but to garner good outcomes from existing partnerships and a steady stream of future partnerships, you must add tangible value.

Finally, the partnering-centric organization has a culture characterized by a flexible, open mindset combined with a strong sense of its own worth and an appreciation for the value of collaborative problem solving. These characteristics are reflected in these comments from a scientific manager in one of these organizations:

> We know we are not the world champions at everything. There's lots we can learn from others, and anyone can have a good idea, not just our own people. But we also know we are good at certain things that we can contribute to our partners, so that when combined, we together can really make things happen.
>
> Each partner is different. It's up to us to adapt to how they work so that we can inject our own competencies effectively and solve difficult scientific problems together.

Compared to the process-driven partnering-savvy companies they frequently collaborate with, partnering-centric organizations may seem to lack clearly defined operating processes and best practices. But this is a misconception. Rather, the in-house processes and practices of the partnering-centric organization focus not on internal effectiveness but on connecting and working effectively with partners' processes, as well as developing and deploying their own competencies for the benefit of partnerships.

Consider, for example, the information technology standards and protocols for data exchange in a drug discovery partnership. The partnering-savvy organization, in pursuit of efficiency and IP protection, will usually seek to host the data on its in-house secure data management system, offering to set up user accounts for external collaborators as needed. The partnering-centric company, on the other hand, will have defined best practices for quickly and efficiently interfacing their own systems with any partner's data repositories and systems or, alternatively, a secure firewall setup that allows their people to log in and work on their partners' systems remotely. As another example, partnering-centric organizations will invest in developing their people's technical, scientific, and commercial competencies specifically in the context of how these skills may be deployed in partnerships.

Alliance Management in Partnering-Centric Organizations

Alliance management is the very essence of the partnering-centric organization; everyone in the company contributes to it. Every partnership will have a specific individual nominated as the partner relationship lead or assigned to some other, similarly designated role. That individual could be someone from the corporate alliance management group, but it is just as likely to be the project leader, a senior member of the project team or a governance committee member. Whoever it is, that person's role is to coordinate other people involved in the partnership who will together fulfill the full range of alliance manager roles and responsibilities. In addition, alliance management will overlap with project management and business development functions in a way that is much fuzzier than it is in traditional companies, or even in partnering-savvy organizations.

In any case, it is important not to get confused by job titles. A partnering-centric organization may not have anyone who is called the alliance manager for a particular partnership, but it still may be conducting alliance management for that partnership extremely well. Conversely some companies (especially those just starting their journeys away from the partnering-tolerant state) have officially designated alliance managers who are not really doing much alliance management at all, at least not in the sense we described in Chapter 9. Instead, they are essentially finance or legal people whose task is to ensure that contractual obligations are being managed, which is a comparatively small part of the overall alliance management role.

A partnering-centric organization may maintain a small corporate alliance management group that, in addition to contributing individuals to work with key partnerships, also actively supports and coaches project leaders and other people responsible for alliance management activities. Since alliance management is viewed as a set of embedded skills and personal competencies, the preferred mechanisms for developing alliance management capabilities are skills training, coaching or mentoring, and community-led small-group experience sharing. This contrasts with partnering-savvy organizations, which tend to see alliance management as a consistent set of processes, practices, and tools.

Examples of Emerging Partnering-Centric Organizations

In contrast to the highly visible activities of emerging partnering-savvy multinationals, the emerging partnering-centric companies are much less obvious to the eye. Many do not even recognize that they are at the leading edge of a new breed of organization.

One biopharma sector that is a natural fit with the partnering-centric approach is the discovery platform technology companies that have set out to become product companies.[1] For example, antibody technology companies such as Ablynx, Genmab, and MorphoSys started as providers of technologies that enabled their partners to generate differentiated drug molecules. Over time, they evolved into hybrid companies that both shared their technologies with other companies via partnerships and developed their own proprietary projects, to be eventually brought to market in partnership with commercial collaborators. As these companies begin to mature, they end up operating a risk-balanced mix of three related but distinct business models:

- Providing their technology (typically via both variants of the IP transfer partnership model) to a variety of collaborators' projects in exchange for royalty and fee-for-service revenues.
- Developing proprietary projects, initially to clinical PoC with the support of CRO and other service provider partners, and subsequently partnering with commercial partners (while retaining at least 50% ownership) to complete the late-stage development programs, gain MAs, and commercialize the resulting products.
- Marketing their own products through partnerships with selected pharma marketers and in some cases operating their own marketing organizations in some geographic territories in collaboration with contract sales service providers. To achieve scale economies, they may in-license products that have synergies with their own marketing activities.

Clearly, such companies must be engaged in scores of different partnerships, in both the research and commercial arenas, and both with other biopharma companies and with service providers, at any one time. Furthermore, they have a comparatively small headcount relative to the scale of the financial flows that their activities control or influence; many people will be working with several different partners at once.

Another biopharma sector that has spawned some emerging partnering-centric companies is the mid-sized pharmaceutical companies, especially those with limited local markets that need to adopt a semi-virtual model in order to compete on a global playing field. Take, for example, Helsinn Healthcare, an archetypal focused biopharma business specializing in cancer supportive care. From its headquarters in Switzerland, Helsinn operates (at the time of writing, in mid-2015) a global business with a portfolio of marketed products in over ninety countries through sixty-five different commercial partners. Its in-house commercial organization specializes in strategic marketing and global product management, although it also maintains its own sales and marketing group in the United States. In R&D, it operates a semi-virtual model to develop and register its own proprietary products with the close support of selected clinical-stage CROs while sourcing new projects through in-licensing from smaller biotech partners or by sponsoring outsourced discovery projects with full-service discovery CROs. Its in-house R&D organization focuses on the relevant therapeutic area and regulatory expertise, R&D program design and steering, and operating collaborative project activities with its co-development and CRO partners.

Using this model, with little more than a hundred R&D people on average in Switzerland and the United States, Helsinn conducted 32 clinical trials between 2012 and 2014, many of them Phase II and III studies, on four different NMEs at almost 900 clinical trial sites involving nearly 8,000 patients, as well as generating several new additional NMEs en route to first human trials. Despite the large number of partnerships implicit in its model, Helsinn does not have a formal corporate alliance management group; rather, alliance management is handled very effectively through the company's commercial, R&D, and project management functions as part of its normal way of doing business.

A second example in the mid-sized pharmaceutical sector is the pharmaceutical R&D organization of Orion Pharma, an archetypal mixed-model pharma marketer. From its headquarters in Finland, Orion (at the time of writing, in mid-2015) operates two main international businesses in proprietary and generic pharmaceuticals, as well as smaller divisions in animal health, medical diagnostics, active pharmaceutical ingredients, and contract manufacturing. Having made a strategic choice to adopt a semi-virtual, open R&D model, Orion has outsourced most of its operational R&D activities in generic product development while focusing its proprietary R&D efforts on the middle of the R&D value chain. It initiates many of its research projects through partnerships with academia and smaller bioscience firms, and then manages the ensuing discovery and development projects through to clinical PoC with the support of CROs. At that point, it partners with larger multinationals to co-develop the products through to registration and subsequent commercialization.

Orion's R&D organization aims to generate a regular flow of assets with clinical PoC at a much higher return on investment than companies with comparable R&D budgets, and by all accounts it is well on the way to achieving this goal. Unlike most other emerging partnering-centric organizations, Orion's current R&D organization is the result of a deliberate effort to create and cultivate a new way of working, consciously and proactively putting in place the key ingredients of a partnering-centric organization; this effort has been documented in the literature.[2] As with Helsinn, Orion does not have a centralized alliance management group; R&D alliance management is handled very effectively as part of the daily work.

A third sector that is spawning partnering-centric organizations is discovery and preclinical CROs that have started to embrace more integrated partnerships with their sponsors, including some risk-and-reward-sharing arrangements. Operating through the sponsored R&D program and joint endeavor partnership models, they are no longer just suppliers or service providers but key participants in collaborative discovery projects with their partners. Examples of such companies (at the time of writing) include not only European and US companies such as Germany's Evotec but also a growing number of Asian firms, such as China's Hutchison Medi Pharma and India's Aurigene.

The Choice between Partnering-Savvy and Partnering-Centric

Looking at the examples in this chapter, you might be tempted to conclude that the process-driven tool-based partnering-savvy approach makes the most sense for a large multinational while the culture-driven mindset-based partnering-centric approach is a better fit for smaller and medium-sized organizations that engage with a wide variety of partners. The reality is not quite as clear-cut as that.

Consider, for example, academic research groups whose main focus is research, publishing, and teaching. It probably does not make sense to manage them as organizations that live and breathe for partnering. A simplified partnering-savvy approach with the help of a few dedicated alliance managers is most likely the best option here.

Or, consider a medium-sized business that has been assembled through multiple acquisitions of smaller organizations. It will be much harder to shape a common partnering culture unless the businesses acquired were very similar in culture. A partnering-savvy approach using processes and tools to ensure consistent partnering behaviors is probably the best option in this case.

The large, multinational pharmas and major global service providers have historically adopted a strong process management and organizational restructuring approach to operationalize their complex matrix structures and to integrate the companies they acquire. The path of least resistance for these companies in their journey to becoming networked R&D organizations is the partnering-savvy approach. This path relies on structural adjustments and a common platform of processes, practices and tools, an approach that aligns well with how these businesses already operate. But that does not mean that the partnering-centric option is closed off to these companies. For example, Eli Lilly's FIPNet (Fully Integrated Pharmaceutical Network) strategy incorporates many elements of a partnering-centric approach.

The necessary culture change is harder to achieve in a very large organization, but is not impossible. At the end of the day, building an organization that excels at operating partnerships requires leadership. And the most appropriate leadership and management styles are somewhat different with respect to the partnering-savvy and partnering-centric approaches. Process and practice driven partnering-savvy organizations are designed and constructed; whereas culture and competence driven partnering-centric organizations are seeded and cultivated.

Thus, the choice to take the partnering-centric route must reflect the senior leadership's appetite for a more distributed style of management that relies on shaping culture and mindset rather than on controlling activities via processes and metrics. In certain project-intensive industries, such as management consulting or information technology services, some of the top-performing companies are indeed culture driven and operate with a large dose of the partnering-centric approach.

In my opinion, there are as yet no fully developed partnering-savvy or partnering-centric organizations, at least not in the biopharma industry. The best of each breed are probably still adolescents, works in progress—there is a lot more to come over the next decade.

Whichever route an organization takes, the ultimate goal is the same—to ensure that partnerships eventually deliver better and more innovative healthcare products. Yes, there is a collaboration tax to pay; partnerships do incur greater costs and risks. But we must not forget that the real reason for building organizations that excel at networked R&D is to improve the state of healthcare and benefit humankind by alleviating suffering and saving lives.

Chapter Notes

[1] For more about this type of business model, see my white paper, "Managing the Strategic Evolution of a Bioscience Platform Company," available at http://scitechstrategy.com/wp-content/uploads/2015/01/PlatformCo-Paper-Jan-15.pdf.

[2] Robert Thong and Timo Lotta, "Creating a Culture of Productivity and Collaborative Innovation: Orion's R&D Transformation," *Research-Technology Management*.58, no. 3 (May–June 2015): 41–50.

GLOSSARY

Numbers in parentheses after a particular term indicates the chapter in which that term first appears. When a definition contains another term in italics, the latter is defined elsewhere in this glossary.

Active pharmaceutical ingredient (API) (2)—The biologically active substance in an approved pharmaceutical *finished dosage form*.

Alliance (1)—Synonym for *partnership*.

Alliance manager (1)—Someone who conducts *alliance management* activities, whether in a dedicated role or as part of other duties and regardless of actual job title.

Alliance management (1)—Those activities carried out to ensure that partnerships proceed efficiently, effectively, and harmoniously to their goals.

Asset-centric company (5)—A very lean entity that serves as a vehicle for developing a specific biopharma asset until it can be sold; there is no intention to create a sustainable long-term business.

Asset-generating engine (5)—A company that reliably and consistently creates a succession of R&D assets at key value inflection points.

Asset partnering strategy (6)—A strategy that defines preferred partnership models and prioritized partner archetypes for a particular shareable asset.

Asymmetric partnership (1)—A *partnership* in which the difference in scale between the parties is very stark, such as one between a small organization and a large, multinational corporation.

Backup pathway (2)—A dormant alternative in the body to the normally active *biological pathway*.

Benefit delivery perspective (1)—An approach that considers a *partnership* through the lens of those factors (besides scientific considerations) that influence the emergence of valuable outputs from the partnership.

Big pharmas (5)—The largest multinational pharmaceutical corporations, typically those with annual sales in excess of US$10 billion.

Bilateral partnership (1)—A *partnership* between two organizations.

Biocluster (1)—A geographic region with a large concentration of bioscience companies and academic institutions creating a bioscience innovation ecosystem.

Bio-dollars (3)—Payments contingent on certain future events or outcomes defined in the partnering agreement; usually used in reference to payments that are less likely to occur.

Biologics (5)—Drug molecules manufactured in biological processes or extracted from biological sources. Typically, they are large, complex proteins.

Biological pathway (2)—A naturally occurring sequence of actions in the body that creates a molecular product, turns genes on or off, or otherwise causes some change at the cellular level.

Biopharma sector (1)—The domain of activity related to researching, innovating, developing, and commercializing new or improved disease therapies, whether through traditional drug development, emerging gene therapies, or some other mechanism.

Biosimilars (5)—A regulator-approved near-identical copy of an original *biologic drug*.

Blockbuster drug (2)—A highly successful drug from a commercial standpoint, with annual sales in excess of US$1 billion while its patents continue to be valid.

Candidate drug (CD) (2)—A prospective new drug molecule that will be tested in clinical trials; once approved by the regulator, it is commonly referred to as the *active pharmaceutical ingredient*.

Chemical manufacturing and control (CMC) activities (5)—Those activities required for the design, development, and scale-up of manufacturing processes for both the *active pharmaceutical ingredient* (also referred to as *drug substance*) and the *finished dosage form* (also referred to as *drug product* or *galenic form*).

Clinical CRO (5)—A provider of services related to clinical trials, including protocol design, patient recruitment, trial monitoring, sample analysis, data management, biostatistics, medical writing, and regulatory advice.

Clinical proof-of-concept (ClinPoC or PoC) (2)—Strong evidence of efficacy in comparatively small Phase II clinical trials with idealized patient samples in combination with acceptable ADME and toxicology data from human and animal testing.

Co-creative joint endeavor (4)—A *joint endeavor* characterized by a deliberate effort to define, plan, and interpret the key experiments of the project together.

Collaboration (1)—A set of activities with planned outcomes and timelines in which two or more organizationally separate parties work with each other to achieve a mutual benefit.

Collaboration management (1)—Synonym for *alliance management*.

Collaboration risk (3)—The incremental risk arising from the added complications of working with one or more external partners, as opposed to executing the project in-house.

Collaboration tax (3)—The additional costs and risks that partnerships bring compared to purely in-house efforts.

Collaborative project (1)—Synonym for *collaboration*.

Collaborative supply arrangement (4)—An arrangement in which the customer participates not only in the design but also in the delivery of customized services from the service provider.

Commercial risk (3)—The risk of the project being unable to meet commercial requirements.

Commodity supplier (4)—A supplier whose customers cannot perceive a difference compared to other suppliers besides price.

Contract research organization (CRO) (1)—Synonym for *R&D service provider.*

Contraindication (2)—Circumstances under which a drug should not be used, such as the presence of a concomitant disease or an allergy.

Corporate alliance management group (1)—A corporate function or group that provides an organizational home for *alliance managers* and also conducts other activities beyond the scope of individual alliance managers, such as managing a portfolio of *alliances.*

Corporate partnering strategy (6)—A strategy that describes the total portfolio of assets available for partnering, sets out in broad terms the role each asset plays in the organization's long-term strategy, and prioritizes assets for partnering.

Cost of goods (COGS) arrangement (3)—Agreement for one party to buy product manufactured by another party based on production costs plus an agreed margin.

Customized supply arrangement (4)—An arrangement in which the service provider incorporates a high degree of value-adding customer specificity into the services provided.

David & Goliath partnership (1)—A *partnership* in which the two parties are mismatched not just in size but also in strategic business aims, operating models, organizational cultures, and relative power.

Deal (1)—The joint decision between the parties to go ahead with a partnership.

Disease variants (2)—A group of diseases that exhibit similar outward symptoms but have different underlying causes at the molecular level.

Divide-and-conquer joint endeavor (4)—A *joint endeavor* in which both parties work concurrently, each with specifically demarcated responsibilities for resources and operational work, and share data and insights at established milestones.

Druggability (2)—The amenability of a *drug target* to having a drug molecule bind to it, including how the physical and chemical characteristics of the drug needed to bind to it affect the practical elements of drug use in humans, such as ADME data.

Drug product (5)—Synonym for *finished dosage form*.

Drug substance (5)—Synonym for *active pharmaceutical ingredient*.

Drug target (2)—A specific molecule in a *biological pathway* for which a drug molecule is created, either to activate it (agonist), block its activity (antagonist), or reverse its activity (inverse agonist).

Due diligence (6)—The formal process before a partnership *deal* is consummated to validate the key assumptions underlying the *term sheet* and other expectations, assess the risks identified in the negotiation process, and uncover other risks that have not been anticipated.

Efficacy (2)—In the drug industry context, whether the drug has an observable impact on the disease symptoms or disease state progression, as measured by disease-specific metrics captured in clinical trials.

Equity (3)—Ownership of shares in a business entity.

Excipients (2)—The non-biologically active substances that are combined with the *active pharmaceutical ingredient* in a specific formulation to produce the *finished dosage form*. The use of appropriate excipients enables long-term stability, ease of administration, and reliable transport in the body to where the active ingredient is needed.

Execution risk (3)—The risk arising from being unable to resolve unanticipated problems or exploit unanticipated opportunities over the course of the project's execution.

Executive champion (7)—In the context of a David & Goliath partnership, a senior-level Goliath person who strongly believes in the value of the partnership for Goliath and advocates for it in Goliath's portfolio management process and other forums.

External collaborative quotient (ECQ) (6)—The extent to which an organization is open to working collaboratively with outsiders and its capacity for doing so.

Finished dosage form (FDF) (2)—The physical form administered to a patient, comprising the *active pharmaceutical ingredient* combined in a specific formulation with other *excipients* to enable long-term stability, ease of administration, and reliable transport within the body to where the active ingredient is needed.

First-in-man (FiM) (2)—The point in the new drug R&D life cycle when the first human clinical trial of the *candidate drug* is initiated.

First-line treatment (2)—The first treatment normally prescribed when the patient is initially diagnosed.

Focused biopharma (5)—An established, financially secure biopharma company with its own focused and distinctive business model and a cultural legacy in R&D or biopharma technology.

Galenic form/formulation (5)—Synonym for *finished dosage form.*

Hands-off sponsored R&D program (4)—A *sponsored R&D program* in which there is essentially no participation by the sponsoring party in the day-to-day work or operational decision making associated with the R&D work.

Health check (8)—A structured process to assess the health and vitality of an ongoing partnership.

Indication (2)—**A** valid reason to use a certain test, medication, procedure, or surgery.

Innovation scouting (10)—The process and practice of finding and initiating new collaborative innovation projects.

IP transfer partnership (4)—A *partnership* where one party transfers previously developed IP to the other for use in one or more of its projects.

Joint endeavor (4)—A *partnership* in which both parties are significantly involved in day-to-day operations and decision making and contribute jointly to value creation and project development.

Key performance indicator (KPI) (8)—A metric used to assess progress and the extent of eventual success for the partnership.

Label (2)—Definition of what the pharmaceutical company is legally allowed by the regulator to promote in terms of a drug's usage, comprising the approved *indication, contraindications,* and other treatment characteristics such as the relevant patient subpopulation, whether the drug is to be used as an initial or *second-line treatment,* and whether it is to be used on its own or in combination with another therapy.

Lead structure/series (2)—The point in the new drug R&D life cycle at which a patentable series of molecules with the same underlying structure from which one or more *candidate drugs* can be derived has been discovered. Also used to refer to such a series of molecules.

Life cycle management (LCM) (2)—The practice of extending a drug's period of exclusivity by gaining approval for a patented variant of the original drug that offers documented performance improvement over the original.

Line extension (2)—Approval of a drug for use in another indication in addition to the original approved indication.

Management reductionism (2)—In the context of R&D, a management philosophy which argues that R&D processes can be regarded as machines that can be engineered to convert specified inputs into predictable outputs, with R&D productivity enhanced through the control of a small number of key management levers.

Marketing authorization (MA) (2)—The product marketing license or other formal permission bestowed by the regulatory authority to allow the marketing of a new drug to the healthcare community. An individual MA is granted for a specific *finished dosage form* with respect to usage according to a specific *label.*

Marketing rights (3)—The rights to promote and sell the final product to end users, usually defined with reference to specific geographic territories.

Mechanism of action (2)—The specific biochemical interaction through which a drug produces its pharmacological effect; usually referred to by the same name as the drug target modulated by that drug.

Milestone payments (3)—Payments made by one party in a partnership to the other at certain points in the project's timeline as defined by agreed success criteria.

Mini-big pharmas (5)—Companies with similar business models and approaches to the *big pharmas* but of somewhat smaller size, typically with annual sales between US$2 and US$8 billion.

Mixed-model pharma marketers (5)—Smaller multinational pharmaceutical companies with a broad mix of related revenue sources ranging across proprietary drugs, generic drugs, drug delivery systems, active pharmaceutical ingredients, consumer health, fine chemicals, medical diagnostics, and contract manufacturing.

Molecular reductionism (2)—In the context of biopharma R&D, a scientific philosophy which argues that disease is best treated by first identifying and then appropriately modulating the action of a single *drug target* along a single *biological pathway*.

Networked R&D (2)—The practice of initiating and operating R&D projects by systematically combining internal resources with those of a network of collaborators and outsourcing providers.

Networked R&D organizations (12)—An organization optimized for *networked R&D.*

New drug application (NDA) (2)—The package of information comprising the formal application to the regulator for a new drug *marketing authorization.*

Nonclinical CRO (5)—A provider of services relating to *in vitro* and *in vivo* experimental studies.

Off-label use (2)—Use of a drug outside of its regulator-approved label; off-label use may be made at the physician's discretion but it cannot be promoted by the marketer.

Off-shoring (5)—The practice of moving operational facilities to lower-cost countries.

Off-target effect (2)—A side effect caused by a candidate drug binding to a different biological molecule than the one it was designed for.

Operational sponsor R&D program (4)—A *sponsored R&D program* in which there is a high degree of day-to-day participation by the sponsor, which may include contributions in kind or involvement in operational-level decision making.

Originator involvement IP transfer (4)—An *IP transfer partnership* in which there is a significant degree of ongoing interaction between the originator and the recipient of the IP.

Over-the-wall IP transfer (4)—An *IP transfer partnership* with minimal interaction once the IP has been transferred.

Partnering-centric organization (12)—An organization that excels at *networked R&D* by integrating partnerships and a partnership mindset deeply into the daily work and culture of the organization to create an altogether new business model.

Partnering-naive organization (12)—An organization having little or no experience of partnering.

Partnering-savvy organization (12)—An organization that excels at *networked R&D* by managing partnerships through specific organizational and operational adjustments to its existing business model.

Partnering-tolerant organization (12)—An organization in which partnerships are viewed as a practical necessity (or even a necessary evil) to be used when a purely in-house project is not viable.

Partnership (1)—Arrangements between the parties in a *collaboration* to allocate and share resources, operating responsibilities, decision making, benefits, and risks, regardless of whether such arrangements have been set out in a formal contract. Can also sometimes be a synonym for *collaboration*.

Pass-the-baton joint endeavor (4)—A *joint endeavor* in which one party conducts all the work up to a certain stage of the project while the other party is kept informed on progress, and then the roles reverse.

Patent cliff (5)—A sharp drop-off in revenue due to the expiration of patents (and ensuing competition from cheap generics) on blockbuster products.

Patient stratification (2)—Processes and tools for identifying the patient subpopulation that suffers from a specific disease variant.

Pay-for-performance (2)—An arrangement between the healthcare payer and the drug manufacturer in which the total cost borne by the payer depends on the drug's effectiveness (measured after treatment) in the overall patient population, usually involving some retrospective adjustment (financial or in kind).

Performance bonus payments (3)—Payments supplementary to *milestone payments* intended to recognize achievement of a milestone at a higher quality or performance level than the minimum defined by the partnership agreement.

Personalized medicine (2)—Synonym for *precision medicine.*

Precedented (2)— Used to describe a *drug target* or *mechanism of action* for which one or more drugs have either already been approved by the regulators, or attractive clinical trial results have been achieved with other candidate drugs.

Precision medicine (2)—A treatment approach based on targeting the underlying cause of a specific disease variant and using that approach in combination with *patient stratification*.

Preferred provider partnership (4)—An arrangement in which a service provider and its customer closely integrate operations, creating cost and time savings for the customer compared to other suppliers of the same services.

Preferred supplier partnership (4)—Synonym for *preferred provider partnership.*

Principal investigator (5)—The senior academic who is ultimately responsible for an academic laboratory's activities and budget.

Product company (5)—A *research-stage biotech* or *focused biopharma* that takes its (at least 50%-owned) projects through late-stage development to product registration, partnering with other companies for worldwide commercialization.

Product innovation partnership (1)—A *partnership* in which participants collaborate to create or develop a product innovation, sharing ownership in the outcome.

Profit share (3)—An arrangement to share the profits (revenues less costs) resulting from the fruits of a partnership.

Project-centric organization (12)—An organization in which projects (as opposed to functional departments) are the focal point of day-to-day work and decision making.

Project champion (7)—In the context of an industry-academic *sponsored R&D program*, the project leader counterpart of the *principal investigator*. In a different context, this term is also sometimes used as a synonym for *executive champion*.

Quality (2)—In the drug industry context, whether the finished dosage form contains the exact same composition of *active pharmaceutical ingredients*, inactive *excipients*, and impurities as was tested in the clinical trials documented for the *new drug application*.

R&D operational funding (3)—The funds needed to cover the operating costs incurred by the partnership as the collaborative project progresses; sometimes called research costs, development costs, or FTE costs.

R&D service provider (5)—A company that provides R&D services to biopharma companies; also known as a *contract research organization.*

Reimbursement level (2)—The proportion of a drug's retail price that is covered by the healthcare payer.

Repurposing (2)—Applying an existing drug to an altogether new indication or disease.

Research-stage biotech (5)—Small and comparatively young company engaged in early-stage biopharma research, often with shorter-term survival challenges and lacking product revenue.

Revenue share (3)—Arrangement to share the revenues resulting from the fruits of a partnership.

Royalty (3)—A payment made by one party for use of intellectual property belonging to another party.

Safety (2)—In the drug industry context, whether the side effects of a drug are medically acceptable at the normally prescribed dosage, as measured initially in animal studies and subsequently in human clinical trials.

Second-line treatment (2)—The treatment normally prescribed as a recourse in case the initial *first-line treatment* does not prove to be effective.

Scientific risk (3)—The risk of the project being unable to achieve its technical aims.

Signing fee (3)—A fee payable from one party to the other at the outset of a partnership, usually in recognition of the value already created by the second party that will be shared.

Small molecule drugs (5)—Traditional drug molecules manufactured through chemical synthesis. They are typically less than 500 daltons in molecular weight, although some antibiotics (produced through chemical synthesis operations on fermented molecules) are still regarded as small molecules despite molecular weights in the region of 700–900 daltons.

Specialist CRO (5)—A *contract research organization* that provides a narrow range of distinctive services that are not available from other CROs.

Specialty marketer (5)—A company marketing specialist products in certain geographic territories with a small, focused sales force.

Sponsored R&D program (4)—An arrangement in which one party funds one or more R&D projects conducted by the other party.

Technology provider (5)—A company that provides specialist IP-protected technology for other companies to use in R&D projects.

Term sheet (6)—A concise summary of the *deal* terms for a prospective partnership, agreed by the parties in negotiation as a basis for the subsequent detailed partnership agreement.

Unprecedented (6)—Used to describe a *drug target* or *mechanism of action* which is not *precedented*.

Value-added outsourcing partnership (1)—A *partnership* in which one party (sponsor) contracts with the other (provider) for customized services or IP-protected technology.

Value-added supply arrangement (4)—Synonym for *value-added supply partnership.*

Value-added supply partnership (4)—A *partnership* in which one party supplies a product or service to the other in a way that adds unique value that would not be created by a *commodity supplier.*

INDEX